meditation
IN A NEW YORK MINUTE

meditation
IN A NEW YORK MINUTE

SUPER CALM
for the
SUPER BUSY

MARK THORNTON

SOUNDS TRUE
Boulder, Colorado

Sounds True, Inc.
Boulder CO 80306
SOUNDS TRUE is a trademark of Sounds True, Inc.

© 2004 Project Bliss and Mark Thornton
All rights reserved. Published 2004, 2006

Printed in Canada

ISBN: 1-59179-429-3

Thornton, Mark
    Meditation in a New York minute: super calm for the super busy / Mark Thornton.
    ISBN 1-59179-429-3
    Library of Congress Control Number: 2005935846

IMPORTANT CAUTION
Although anyone may find the practices, disciplines, and understanding in this book to be useful, it is sold with the understanding that neither the author nor Sounds True are engaged in presenting specific medical, psychological, emotional, or spiritual advice. Nor is anything in this book intended to be a diagnosis, prescription, recommendation, or cure for any specific kind of medical, psychological, emotional, or spiritual problem. Each person has unique needs and this book cannot take these individual differences into account. Each person should engage in a program of treatment, prevention, cure, or general health only in consultation with a licensed, qualified physician, therapist, or other competent professional. Any person suffering from severe stress, anxiety, depression, worries, and concerns should consult with a medical doctor and licensed, qualified psychologist or therapist before practicing the methods described in this book.

This book is dedicated to the
wild, untamed passion of
Your Heart
which contains within
all the gods you will ever need.

What are you talking about?

Having to earn a living
Doesn't stop you digging for the Treasure.
Don't abandon everyday life.

That's where the Treasure is.

RUMI

Table of Contents

ACKNOWLEDGMENTS

I would like to honor all the teachers from whom
I have learned, for their secrets and their passion
in turning me back to the source.

To my parents who have suffered through my
strange career shift from investment banker to
meditation teacher. To my friends who have seen
all of this unfold. And to the Divine, whose heart
searches for me everywhere.

By the end of this book you will have tools
to create calm and connectedness

Anywhere

Anytime

Imagine a world where you could:

De-stress effortlessly

•

Feel centered no matter what

•

Easily create an oasis of calm anywhere in your day

•

Feel powerfully connected to life

•

Begin to perceive stress as optional

All without changing anything from your busy schedule!

Introduction

Our lives are lived at warp speed.

Our hectic schedules are crammed with crises, to-do lists, issues marked urgent and overflowing in trays, unpaid bills, a sea of unread email, and deadlines with due dates close to last Christmas. Our agendas have everything in them but "relax." Whether an executive, single mother or factory worker, we have all been affected by the increased pace and complexity of life. More than ever, we need to create calm quickly and profoundly. We need to feel connected to life, in the middle of our frantic days.

What's the solution?

The secret is centuries old. We can do more by relaxing more. We can go faster by slowing down more frequently. Deep inside yourself, now, lies a space that is always calm. Far away from everyday events, at your core, lies a place of quiet, calm, serenity, and stillness. Even by reading these words you can begin to relax and journey to the mystical place that sages and saints call the "ocean of calm." The goal of *Meditation in a New York Minute* is to show you how to access this place whenever you need to. Feeling connected to life and your core can be an everyday and effortless activity. **It's not just possible;**

it's the way it should be. You can be super busy, super successful, *and* super calm at the same time. No matter what you do, there are simple, quick, and sure-fire ways to swim in the ocean of calm.

Formula One racing cars need frequent pit stops; otherwise they run out of fuel. Your mind also needs to slow down quickly to refuel, before speeding up again. By the time you've finished reading this book, you will have tools you need to access the ocean of calm, like a pit stop, to reenergize, gain perspective, enliven your spirit, and head out again—all in less than a New York minute!

Let me give you an example from my own life. As an investment banker my days were often fourteen hours long, and I frequently worked six-day weeks. The more successful my career, the more I needed meditation to relax quickly. In my experience, stress reduced my performance at work, led to poor decision making, reduced mental clarity, and increased levels of frustration. During this time, I used up to nineteen meditations that could be done in less than a New York minute to remain focused, calm, to make better decisions, to respond from my core values, and to get the job done, effortlessly.

I trained with a number of meditation masters over twenty-two years and learned a range of techniques to relax effortlessly, deeply, and, above all, quickly. I was amazed to find that even as a busy C.O.O. I was able to meditate for a total of an hour each workday, without changing anything from my daily schedule.

Let me repeat that: *I was able to meditate for a total of an hour each workday, without changing anything from my daily schedule.*

I still kept all my work hours. I attended the same meetings. I didn't have to leave early from or arrive late at work to meditate. I didn't have to sacrifice "time at the gym" or "relaxing with friends" to become calm. Specifically, I learned ways to create calm while moving about in the world, without setting aside time to sit cross-legged in a quiet room. If this sounds impossible, read on!

In my work as an executive meditation coach, I've found that even the most successful people have one to two hours a day they can spend creating calm, building energy, and de-stressing. For example, even the busiest people shower in the morning, commute to work, have lunch, sit in the backs of taxis, walk down streets, have moments before and after meetings, walk from meetings to other meetings, and travel home from work. All are profound opportunities to experience calm.

My new career has been teaching major corporations about finding calm. I've spent more than 3,000 hours learning and teaching these techniques in the past year alone. After I left JPMorgan I spent a year with thirty different spiritual teachers, in more than seven different countries, to find the best techniques for Super Busy people. In the past five years alone, I've done more than 5,000 hours of learning and teaching meditation. I've been exploring meditation for more than twenty-two years and created meditation groups in New York, London, and Melbourne.

This book describes nineteen techniques to access the ocean of calm whenever and wherever you are. The meditations cover a range of situations in which you may find yourself. You'll find all you need to identify the parts of your busy schedule that can be used to create calm.

This book is unashamedly aimed at those people who need solutions fast! The layout is designed to give the ideal amount of information with maximum results. It aims to be as easy and effective as aspirin.

We are not attempting surgery here; we aim to relieve the symptoms of stress rather than the causes.

As a result, philosophy and theology are largely ignored. Your capacity to discuss comparative religions at dinner parties will be unchanged. Meditation is a tool, like a hammer, with a specific purpose. The purpose of this book is to quickly get you to the ocean of calm and explore the techniques and find what works.

There are three parts to the book:

The Journey

The Essentials

The Techniques

Your pay-off from the book will increase threefold if you read the entire book. For those new to meditation, the first two sections contain all you need to know to practice with ease (Laws, Secrets, and Useful Ideas). For those with many years of meditating experience, the invitation is to deepen and stretch your capacity to meditate. Each technique has tips, frequently asked questions, and common challenges.

Explore these techniques; see what works. Try them in different situations. Find the combination of techniques that perfectly suits your needs, your schedule, and the pull of your heart. Being calm and connected in your everyday life isn't just possible; it's the way it should be.

My personal goal is to turn you on to the awesome power that lies within your center—your heart.

THE BENEFITS

This book provides the process, guidelines, and building blocks to create an oasis of calm in your everyday life, not just in spite of your everyday life. It offers proven ways to:

- Improve health
- Lower stress
- Work with an open and relaxed body
- Feel connected and alive to life

Generally you will be able to:
- Deal with stress more effectively
- Improve your sense of well-being
- Meditate for at least an hour every day
- Learn techniques that promote no dogma, doctrine, spiritual discipline, or school of spiritual thought

Specifically you will learn:
- Five powerful tools to dynamically multiply the benefits of your meditation
- Eight Laws of Meditation that apply to effectively creating calm
- Eleven of the most common traps and how to successfully avoid them
- Seven guidelines to effectively direct and make your journey easy
- Nineteen sure-fire, easy-to-use techniques to do in a New York minute (Each technique contains a wealth of tips, and common challenges and how to avoid them.)

Screensaver Reminder
To prepare for calm, change the screensaver on your PC at work and your laptop. These are reminders to practice the techniques in this book. Some executives have "Deep Calm" others have "Breathe" and others "Calm."

what's possible

"How come you look so *calm"?*

It was the middle of one of the busiest days in my fourteen year career ... chaos reigned, staff were threatening to leave, critical deadlines were being missed, my boss in Geneva was furious, and our biggest clients were about to jump ship. Most of these problems were directly related to my area, so I was surprised at the question.

I realized I *was* calm, in the middle of all this. Not because I didn't care about the result, or because I was comatose and asleep under my desk. I hadn't given up, and I wasn't about to go on holiday. I wasn't burying my head ostrich style in the sand and hoping everything was going to blow over. I realized with surprise that the main reason was the constant use of nineteen different meditation techniques that I used ...

Everyday

Anywhere

Anytime

My surprise was that the techniques had become second nature to me. They had become a habit that took as much effort as tying my shoelaces. They had become a natural and essential part of my day.

HOW TO MAKE THE MOST OF THIS BOOK

How much you get from this book depends on how much you put into it.

Imagine a person who has never previously played golf arriving at the first hole with all the right equipment. He opens a book entitled *How to Play Golf*. He skim reads the pages and concludes, "It's easy—it's just hitting a ball into a hole." He takes a club and starts to swing. Clumps of earth are launched down the fairway. The golfer decides more effort is required and swings with more vigor than before. Divots appear, more sods of earth are sent skyward, and generally the golfer appears to be digging his way to China. The golfer then concludes, "Golf is hopeless."

A far more sensible approach is to invest time in reading the entire book, studying each of the techniques and all of the FAQs, common challenges, and solutions. Then it is sensible to practice at home, to take a few gentle swings in the backyard before stepping onto the golf course. Ultimately, the benefits depend on how positive and practiced the player is.

It's like learning any sport—how long before the forward or linebacker or goalkeeper masters the game depends on how much he or she puts into it.

PREMISES FOR THIS BOOK

This book is designed for a certain audience. See if the following applies to you:

- You are a busy person.
- You have an interest in meditation but do not have a great deal of time.
- You want stuff that works now!
- You have a preference for action and quick results over theory/ philosophy.
- You are successful and know there is something more, even though you may not know what "more" is.
- You are more likely to wear a suit than beads, sarongs, and kaftans.
- You are currently more familiar with laptops, PCs, cell phones, and

personal organizers than the inside of temples, shrines, mosques, ashrams, and quiet country retreat centers.

If the above is true, then this book is for you!

THE QUICK FIX?

Admit it. We're all tired of claims about instant this, and instant that. Simply watching an infomercial is enough to close any heart. So I'll be honest—this is not a quick-fix book. I am encouraging readers to meditate for up to an hour each day, every day. For most people, that is a significant increase in daily meditation time. That's twenty-eight hours a month, without changing anything from their schedules. Also, there are nineteen techniques; some will take a life-time to master.

Let me repeat that, in case you are skim reading: *There are nineteen techniques—some will take a lifetime to master.* Some of these techniques are practiced by Zen monks in monasteries, and few of them would claim to have "mastered" them. All the techniques can be done in sixty seconds or less. However, as with new parents learning about raising a child, mastery doesn't happen overnight.

THE CALM HEART

Let's Get Calm

Remember a time when you felt totally relaxed. Where were you? Perhaps it was watching a sunset. Or walking in nature. Maybe it was on vacation on a tropical island where you allowed everyday stresses to simply drift away. Close your eyes and remember that time; try to remember what scents, sensations, and experiences were there. What feelings of relaxation washed over you? How relaxed did your body feel? Whatever memory you now experience, give yourself permission to experience this experience again.

Place your hand on the place in your body where you experience these sensations the most. It may be that you now have a more relaxed feeling in your forehead, or that your breathing has slowed as you remember the feeling of calm. Perhaps you experience a feeling of delight and ease in your chest area as you remember the waves lapping by the seashore on your last vacation.

Now keep your hand on the place on your body where you notice these sensations the most and look at the symbol below—the heart.

Throughout this book I will insert this symbol to slow down your reading, as Super Busy people tend to skim read. This symbol will remind you take a breath and remember your experience of calm. Every time you notice this symbol, allow yourself to deeply relax.

IT'S ABOUT YOU

This entire book is about you. You are unique. No one has had your exact background, your distinct features, your personality or smile. In fact, everything about you has nuances and quirks that make you individual. Meditation is simply a journey to the center of this uniqueness, your core, effortlessly. It's a journey to a part of you often hidden by the noise and busyness of our days.

This book will help you choose meditation tools that perfectly fit your lifestyle, specific goals, unique pressures, that make your heart sing and above all work in a New York minute! With this book in hand, you can start to feel better about relaxing in everyday situations.

Whichever path you choose will be your very own.

YOUR CENTER

Meditation is a journey to the ocean of calm. As you read these words, you can slip into the ocean of calm at any time. An amazing truth about the ocean of calm, deep inside yourself, is that it has many different layers. As you sink deeper into the calm, you come across layers of love, bliss, compassion, joy, delight, and a range of other fragrances and textures. Deep beneath all of these lies your heart.

What is your heart? How do we get there? Why would we really want to do this?

I'm not referring to your physical heart, which pumps blood throughout your body. Nor to the center of your chest, which some traditions refer to as a center of energy called the *heart chakra*. Nor to "heart" in the Buddhist sense, which is located in the mind. All of the above are just doorways into a deeper part of you. Your heart, as in the phrase "the heart of the matter," is your essence, your center, your core.

But you know all of this already. You already know your heart, because it's the:

- Feeling you had when you fell in love
- Experience of a sunset whose beauty brought you to stillness
- Powerful intuition that turned out to be correct

- Most profound moment of prayer
- Deepest experience of meditation
- Emotion you felt when seeing inspiring art
- Sensation you had when you read a life-changing book
- Moment you witnessed the birth of a child

Your heart contains your:
- Wildest dreams
- Deepest longings
- Innermost secrets
- Core values
- Essence, the very source of your uniqueness

Your heart is the place where:
- Creativity is born.
- Inspiration finds its voice.
- Wisdom whispers its secrets.
- The footprints of God are seen.
- The heartbeat of the universe is felt.
- The fragrance of love can be smelled.
- The sweetness of compassion can be tasted.
- The texture of what is eternal can be touched.
- The endless journey into yourself begins.

I Am Calm
This is a mantra technique:
With each in-breath say to yourself "I AM ... "

With the out breath say "C A L M." Repeat this five times. Notice which parts of your body feel more relaxed, open, quiet, still, and calm.

A mantra is a sacred word or syllable that is repeated, out loud or inwardly, in order to achieve a certain effect. Scientific research has proven that ancient techniques such as mantras powerfully create calm.

Imagine what it would be like to live from this place, to have these qualities available to you at any moment. You are just minutes away from experiencing sure-fire ways to experience your core.

SUMMARY

The ocean of calm is within.

The ocean of calm has many layers, such as love, bliss, joy, and compassion.

Deeper than all of this lies your heart, your essence, your core.

You are Super Busy and need techniques that work.

By reading these words, you will learn ways to relax.

PART ONE

The Journey

In this section you will answer these questions:

Why meditate … and why now?

●

Where is this phenomenal ocean of calm?
How can I get there?

●

What's the astonishing difference between calm and Super Calm?

●

How deep will my journey to the ocean of calm be?

You will learn the amazing ancient secret of transforming:

Chaos	$\longrightarrow$	Calm
Noise	$\longrightarrow$	Silence
Activity	$\longrightarrow$	Stillness
Effort	$\longrightarrow$	Effortlessness

Why Meditate ... and Why Now?

You may wonder whether meditation has any application in your world. Perhaps you think meditation is a practice only for people who have renounced the outside world and can afford to spend hours each day sitting silently.

But the truth of the matter is, we need meditation now more than ever. The practice of meditation can help you reduce the stress that all of us feel as a result of the hectic pace of modern life. With the techniques in this book, you can remain calm and centered no matter what challenges your workday presents, and you can practice these techniques without changing your already busy schedule.

And guess what? When you remain calm and centered, the world is a different place. When stressful situations arise, the skills learned in meditation allow you to let go of the anger, frustration, and obsessive thoughts that so often arise as a result of stress.

Yet stress is so much a part of daily life that we often don't even see its subtle and far-reaching effects. We don't see how it makes us feel disconnected from our hearts and robs our life of joy. The book you hold in your hands contains all the tools you need to transform that stress into calm.

THE CURSE OF THE 60,000: AN EXERCISE

What's the first thought when you first wake up in the morning? When you at last get to bed? Do you wake up full of aliveness and delight? Or do you feel tension, stress, worry, and concern?

At a seminar for a Fortune 100 company, I led participants in the following exercise. It's simply an attempt to identify the content of your mind. Here's what I'd like you to do. Take out a pen and paper and do a quick brainstorm of your most common thoughts. Obviously you have good and bad experiences, but what are the *most common* things you think about *every day?* What do you think about when you walk down the street? Or on your commute? Or when you walk to get lunch?

Once you've jotted down some of your common thoughts, I'd like you to look for the common threads or categories of thoughts. For example, if you are frequently anxious about something on your to-do list, write down "Anxious" as the category. If you are worried about picking up the dry cleaning, then write "Worried." If you're afraid about your job prospects, write down "Afraid."

Take a few minutes to quickly write down your list.

Here's the list the executives in the seminar provided:

Stress	Tension	Unconfident
Anxious	Depressed	Aloneness
Lack of Peace	Concern	Worry
Sadness	Anger	Frustration
Helpless	Joy	Rage
Terror	Unease	Fearful
Wary	Constantly Vigilant	

This is quite a depressing list. These were highly successful business people, and yet these negative categories of thought were what most commonly filled their minds. This is what preoccupied them when they woke up, walked down the street, or commuted to work. Although one woman wrote "Joy," on closer questioning it was not an *everyday* state of being. It's depressing just looking at it. But it gets worse.

You have 60,000 thoughts a day. That means you think the above thoughts 60,000 times every day. That's not the most depressing thing. The thoughts you think today are largely the same thoughts you thought yesterday. And the day before.

Take the above list and multiply it by 60,000. Now multiply that list by seven days a week. Then multiply that by fifty-two weeks. Multiply that by your age.

If your list is anything like those of the executives I worked with, then your daily condition is one of constant negative thoughts. Is there a way out of this mental trap?

Luckily for all of us, there is. The pattern of negative thoughts is precisely the condition this book solves. *Meditation in a New York Minute* is designed to give you micro-breaks from these thoughts of sixty seconds or less to not only break up this cycle, but to create a brand new cycle of calm, ease, and delight.

THE WAY YOU *SHOULD* FEEL

I believe your most common everyday experiences should be categories like:

Relaxed	Centered	Grounded
Confident	Peaceful	Calm
At Ease	Delighted	Open

This should be your natural state. Using micro-breaks, your walk down the street can be filled with "Calm," rather than "Stress." When you wake up in the morning, there can be a sense of "Ease" rather than "Anxiousness." Your commute can be "Relaxed" rather than "Fearful."

But that would be just "Calm." This book is called "Super Calm." In creating Super Calm, "Love, Bliss, Joy, Compassion, Delight, Power" can be your *most common* everyday experiences. And *that's* the answer to the question, "Why meditate?"

Three Quick Tips for Calm

Notice if you are clenching your jaw. For the next five minutes, allow the muscles in your jaw to relax. Notice ten times throughout the day if your jaw has become clenched and tight. Less tension here makes you feel less stressed.

Place a finger in the middle of your eyebrows. Lower your head forward so your chin is close to your chest. Close your eyes, and focus your eyes on your finger tip for one minute. It's fine if your eyelids flutter. This breaks the pattern of stressful thoughts and creates calm.

Take your cell phone. Change the welcome display to "Calm Now" or "Breathe!" or "Super Calm Now!" This will be a constant reminder to practice creating calm.

the post 9/11 world

"People are searching for more meaning."

The speaker, a mother of three children, held down a busy Wall Street job as well. It was the end of a meditation seminar.

"They are looking for more ..." the speaker hesitated again, "... connection."

"To what?" I asked.

After an even longer pause, she replied, "To people. To life."

I was surprised at the way she responded. She was a managing director for a major investment firm. She was a native New Yorker. I had worked with her for a number of years and had never heard her speak about such issues. In the banking world, talking about these sorts of things was uncommon. The horror of 9/11 and the shock it sent through the hearts of the people has left America changed.

"New Yorkers have changed," she continued. "We seem to sense that life is more precious than before. There is an awareness ..." her voice trailed off as she tried to find the right words, "that we need to make more of the time we have left."

Her comments and openness intrigued me. In a way her remarks raised more questions than they answered. "More connection—but to which people? Make more of this life—but how? Make more of the precious time—but how?"

I asked her to clarify.

"For a few of us, we simply want to stop and smell the roses. Spend time with loved ones, our family, and friends. For most of us, it's also raised questions about what and who we really value. For a few others, it's a search for new meaning."

This book does not have the answer to any of these questions. Nor does it recommend a certain approach. The answer will be different for each person.

This book shares only where the answer can be found ... at the core of your being.

THE NEW REALITY

The digital age, with all its technological revolutions, has brought us more of everything—more responsibilities, more work, and more stress. In fact, we receive more information in one day than a person in the Renaissance received in a lifetime. In today's hectic world, there is more reason than ever to tap into the power of ancient meditation techniques to create calm. So, just how big a problem is stress in our daily lives?

- A recent survey revealed 80 percent of Americans feel "stressed or very stressed." (*The New York Times*)
- One in every six Americans suffers from depression and anxiety. (*The New York Times*)
- Executives spend significantly more quality time per week with their computers than with their families.
- Stress related illness costs the U.S. 10 percent of gross national product each year. (*The Financial Times* of London)
- An official Australian government report predicts that by the year 2010, the number one reason for visiting a general practitioner will be non-medical, i.e., due to stress, anxiety, and depression.
- A company in Tokyo rents dogs to executives to pet in order to calm themselves before work in the afternoon. (*Campaign* magazine)

STRESS IMPACTS THE BOTTOM LINE

Even companies are realizing the need to create calm:

- American Airlines claims that absenteeism costs the company one million dollars *a day.* (*The Wall Street Journal*)
- Industry loses approximately 550 million workdays annually due to absenteeism. (*The New York Times*)

- The majority of U.S. states have passed laws allowing employees to sue for having stressful conditions. (The National Institute of Occupational Safety and Health)

- A recent health study found that people with prolonged work stress suffer an increase in blood pressure equivalent to aging fifteen years. (Cornell University)

- In one major financial institution, depression was responsible for nearly 11,000 lost workdays over a two-year period (more than high blood pressure and diabetes, combined). (The National Institute of Occupational Safety and Health)

- 42 percent of office workers claim they work in an office where "yelling and verbal abuse happen frequently." (Survey, The Marlin Company)

- Nearly one in three adults experiences high stress every day. (*The Overworked American: The Unexpected Decline of Leisure*)

- The National Institute of Occupational Safety and Health says "stressful working conditions are ... associated with increased absenteeism, tardiness, and intention by workers to quit their jobs—all of which have a negative effect on the bottom line."

As the pace and complexity of life expand exponentially, the need to experience the ocean of calm increases. No single technique is enough. The velocity and intensity of our lives require a range of different tools to help us remain focused and enlivened. While meditation will not solve the cause of stress, it powerfully deals with the symptoms.

The Open Fist

Breathe in and clench your right hand into a fist. Close your eyes. Breath out slowly and relax your fist open. Do this five times.

THE CONDITION YOU ARE ABOUT TO OVERCOME: A QUIZ

Take a moment to answer these questions to identify the amount of stress you have in your life.

Do you take work home?   Yes___   No___

Are you a perfectionist?   Yes___   No___

Would you rather be at work?   Yes___   No___

Do you have difficulty taking a compliment?   Yes___   No___

Do you spend more time at your computer than with your loved ones?   Yes___   No___

Do you generally have more than 20 unread emails every day? Yes___   No___

Is your to-do list longer than one page?   Yes___   No___

Are there more than five items with due dates that have passed? Yes___   No___

When you come home, do you still think and plan strategies for work?   Yes___   No___

When you take a break at work, are you still contactable by cell or pager?   Yes___   No___

Do you check the Internet via PDA, cell, or wi/fi on your break? Yes___   No___

When you greet your loved ones and family at night, are work issues still bubbling away in the background?   Yes___   No___

On your annual holidays, does it generally take more than one week to really unwind?   Yes___   No___

When you lie in bed, do thoughts race through your mind? Yes___   No___

Do you feel panic, concern, or urgency when you wake up in the morning?   Yes___   No___

Do you ever think, "All I need is just one month, then I could clear everything and be back to my normal self again"? Yes___   No___

Do you suffer from any of the following: headache, back pain, emotional fatigue, physical fatigue?   Yes___   No___

Are you experiencing low self-esteem?   Yes___   No___

Is your attitude becoming increasingly negative?   Yes___   No___

Do you have a sense of "What am I doing in life?" Yes___   No___

Do you have non-specific aches, pains, rashes, chest pains, or other illnesses?   Yes___   No___

Are you looking for a greater sense of purpose?   Yes___   No___

Are you daydreaming about escaping from it all?   Yes___   No___

Are you the last to leave your desk at night and/or the first at the office in the morning?   Yes___   No___

Have you ignored hobbies in favor of more time at work? Yes___   No___

If you answered Yes to more than ten questions, relax—you are not alone. It simply means the busy have grown into the Super Busy—always on the go.

THE STRESS TEST

Let's try this simple exercise to identify the amount of stress you are carrying in your body right now. The basic principal is that your tendons, muscles, fascia, and tissues tighten and contract when you experience stress. There are many other ways to measure stress (i.e., via EEG machines, monitoring blood pressure, respiratory rate, heart rate, levels of stress hormones such as cortisol). Without such equipment, you can check the amount of tension by carrying out the following:

- Notice the muscles in your shoulders. See if there is any tension there. You may want to hunch your shoulders toward your ears and then relax them to get an idea of your level of stress.

- Notice the small muscles around your eyes. Allow them to relax. You may need to squint, blink, and even gently massage this area to really allow them to relax.

- Now allow the muscles in your forehead to relax. Again you may want to put the book down and gently massage your forehead and your temples.

- Now notice the muscles in your neck. If it is safe to do so, gently allow your head to roll from side to side.

- Notice your jaw muscles. Deliberately soften the jaw and allow it to loosen and remain gently open.

- Now notice the muscles in your belly. To do this, take one deep and full breath from your belly. Take another deep breath, this time while keeping your chest and shoulders still—this allows more air into your belly. Take one more deep breath and use your abdominal muscles to actually push the belly out. Then relax and notice whether there is a greater sense of ease and relaxation in your stomach muscles.

Most people are amazed at the level of tension they are carrying, especially given the task (reading this book) they (and you) are carrying out. If you think about this logically, there is no need to keep your belly tight—it will not help you assimilate information faster. There is no need to tighten the muscles in your forehead, stomach, or jaw—it will not improve your enjoyment of reading. Although I'm making gentle fun of this, it does seem strange how familiar we have become with tension. *We expect it.*

"So what's wrong with a bit of tension?" I hear you say. Holding onto tension for five minutes, there's no problem. Even for days, weeks, or months, there is no problem. But as the default setting for every day of your life and every activity of your life, this is an entirely unnecessary burden on the health of your body. Your system is operating in fight or flight syndrome even during a relaxing activity such as reading. Energy is diverted to keeping muscles, which could be used for other purposes, tight. Extra adrenaline is required, our immune system becomes weaker over time, and we work harder for simple pleasures.

Tension has become our default setting.

the boiling frog

There is a story about scientists who conducted an experiment with a frog. They placed it in a pot of water and over a long period of time slowly increased the temperature. A frog's memory is so short it has nothing by which to remember the temperature of more than a few minutes ago. As the temperature rose, the frog believed the higher temperature was normal. Eventually it boiled to death.

THE DOWN SIDE OF BEING SUPER BUSY

In the meditation courses I run for executives, many of them complain of similar symptoms:

- "I just feel more stressed."
- "My ability to really relax and enjoy my weekends has gone."
- "Nothing specific is wrong. I just feel less alive than before."
- "Thoughts race through my mind at night."
- "I feel less connected to life."
- "Life seems full of too much static, too much 'noise.'"
- "It's harder to see the woods for the trees."
- "I feel swamped with tasks—everything is passing by in a blur."
- "I can't leave my work at work. I bring it home as well. Not just in my briefcase, but emotionally."
- "I feel I want to take a year off. Not to follow my passion, but to find it."

None of these people lack success, drive, or the capacity to be successful. All they lack are tools to access the ocean of calm. OK, you got that. So let's begin our journey—now!

A Deep Breath

Count your in-breath for four seconds. Hold for one second. Breathe out to the count of four. Allow your in-breathing to be deep and full.

2

Journey to Your Heart

Meditation is a journey to the ocean of calm. Swimming in the ocean of calm you can deal with deadlines with ease, be less stressed on your commute, and do your job with less effort. It is a journey to your center, your core—the place that holds your essence, your deepest longings, your wildest dreams, what nourishes you most, and what you value most. Some people call it spirit, soul, true nature.

The analogy used by Maharishi Mahesh Yogi, the founder of Transcendental Meditation, is that you are like the ocean. At the moment you are standing on the shore looking out onto the ocean, you see only the surface activity of the ocean—the waves, the reflection of the sun—and you can hear the sound of the waves crashing on the shore. Meditation is a journey into the ocean and away from the surface into the deepest depths of you.

The journey within can be as daunting as a first-time trip to a foreign country. As on most journeys, you will need a map, a compass, a destination, tales about the obstacles you will face, some rules about safety, signposts to show you the way, advice on some of the delights you can expect and the wisdom of others who have made the same journey before you.

- The book is a map that outlines a number of paths.
- Your heart is the compass—only your heart will know what is right.
- The destination is your heart.
- The Eleven Thieves are the obstacles you can expect to meet on the path.
- The Eight Laws of Meditation are the rules.
- The Seven Meditation Paths are the signposts.
- The Seven Sages are the wisdom of others.

Perfect Calm

Close your eyes and remember a time of perfect calm in your life. Feel the sensations, hear the sounds, and see the scene. Now declare "I radiate perfect calm to all I meet."

Let me give you an example.

THE HEART

Meditation is simply a way to get to your heart. We can represent this in the diagram below. This diagram is a rough approximation at best, but a helpful guide. There are many other models of how we are structured.

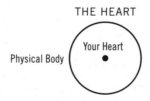

The circumference represents the physical body—the body you can see, feel, taste, hear, and smell. It represents the surface of your being, like the surface of the ocean. There is quite a dense, solid, and heavy quality to it.

Your heart is at the center of the circle and represents the deepest part of your being. Studying this diagram, you can begin to see how your body is similar to the surface of the ocean, and that your core lies deeper than this.

Said another way, your center remains still and calm—undisturbed by the surface events, noises, and distractions of your life. In the same way the depths of the ocean remain calm and unaffected by surface storms.

In this way, meditation allows you to shift from chaos to calm, noise to silence, activity to stillness.

Let's deepen this experience. As you sink deeper inside yourself, you notice two other "bodies," other than your physical body. These are your thinking body (or mind), which is your capacity to think, and your emotional body, which is your capacity to experience emotion.

YOUR PHYSICAL AND EMOTIONAL BODY

In this diagram, the mind is seen as "deeper" than the physical body, indicating that it belongs to the inner world. Once you leave the surface of the ocean, you journey into your inner world. For example, a thought is still a "thing." It is distinct. It is as an object in that you can perceive it, but it has a different quality to it than the external world. It is not something you can pick up. It's quality is more subtle, more etheric. A thought is simply a subtle form of energy.

The same with emotions. You certainly know you have emotions, and they are "real" in that sense. However, because they belong to your inner world, they have a more subtle, less dense, less solid quality than an object in the physical world.

Meditation is your journey through the layers of mind and emotion. Your journey to the core, therefore, is a journey from dense to subtle, from solid to subtle, from the physical world where you need your five senses (sight, touch, taste, hearing, and smell), to your core, which cannot be perceived by these five senses.

Imagine you are swimming in the ocean. Imagine lying on your back on the surface looking up at the sky. Imagine allowing yourself to sink—away from the surface, from the sunlight, from the gentle breeze, from the sound of the wind—and drift down. The first thing you would experience is the world of thoughts—often millions of thoughts racing inside your mind. As you continued to drift further inside, you would find what feelings and emotions were inside you—those of which you may not have been aware when you were lying on your back on the surface. This is the layer of emotions. Meditation is sinking deeper beneath both these layers into the still, silent place within you that is always calm.

Storms can rage on the surface, but your center is always calm.

The following diagram illustrates that meditation is the path to your heart.

THE PATH TO YOUR CORE

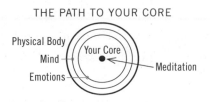

THE ENDLESS JOURNEY AND THE CENTERLESS CENTER

The more you journey to your center, the more you discover that your center is not a single destination. It is not one specific geographical place. The more you dive into the ocean, the more you discover that the edges of who you are, are less rigid than you thought. The deeper you go, the more you see that who you are is actually bigger than you thought. At your deepest, there is no difference between who you are and who others are. The experience of being separate starts to disappear. The idea of "you" and "me" becomes blurred. From this space, the seeds of compassion arise. Any action that would be detrimental to another is experienced as being detrimental to the whole.

The diagram on the next page is the same diagram above seen from a different angle. The same three bodies (physical, mental, and emotional) are there, but the destination of "your center" has a question mark next to it. Like trying to find the center of the ocean, we find there is no such place. There is simply a vast and endless depth into which you dive further, a depth in which the journey becomes an end in itself. The journey becomes the destination. The true nature of your core is that it is vast and endless. No matter how many times you explore your heart, there is always more. It has no center because it's too vast and extends into all things.

One of my teachers asked a holy Indian saint about his experience in journeying into his heart. This profound saint replied, "There is always more. Today at eighty years of age, and after journeying to my heart in every moment since I was twelve, I can honestly say that the journey is endless." My teacher was amazed to hear such a response.

THE CENTERLESS CENTER

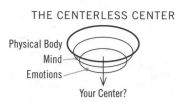

Hold on—what's it like at the center? Why would we want to journey there in the first place?

As you journey to your center, eventually the qualities that exist there (wisdom, love, inspiration, creativity, intuition, calm) start to flow out into the world. It's as if the frequent journey into your heart creates pathways that allow the center to flow outward—effortlessly.

HEART QUALITY FLOWS OUTWARD

Like a river, the qualities from your heart can flow powerfully from the inner to the outer world. Imagine what it would be like if your deepest longings, strongest intuitions, fiercest loves, most passionate desires, bottomless compassion, wildest dreams, highest truths, your core values flowed out into the world. When you meet people, compassion could be the quality you exude rather than self-interest. As the idea of separation starts to melt, narrow self-centeredness becomes less of an option. You get to be heart-centered rather than self-centered. As you sit on the subway, the qualities of your heart can be available to you. When you meet people for the first time, your heart can speak rather than your judgments. Your words can have the quality of depth, love, compassion, and wisdom all because of your connection to your essence or heart. Decisions at work can come from your core values, rather than grasping self-interest. The way you are at work, from your relationship with your boss to your relationship with clients, can come from a deeper sense of teamwork, service, and emotional intelligence.

What does this mean for the Super Busy? When you talk on your cell phone, you can feel the quality and energy of your heart. When you walk down the street on your way to work, you can feel the current of your heart, like the currents, tides, and swell of the ocean. When you meet people, you can connect with their hearts. Perhaps inspiration moves you in new ways. Maybe creativity comes alive in you in ways that you couldn't imagine. Can your relationships be colored by the texture, fibers, and fragrance of your heart? Could your relationships with your loved ones deepen the quality of love that you've always known was inside you? Can love finally flow freely, no longer blocked by the surface drama of your days? The still, quiet power of your heart gets to move about in the world, creating its blessings for all you meet. Maybe people sense something's changed in you, although they may never know what that is. The scent and fragrance of your heart, its uniqueness, its rare quality, can flow out into the world.

This is my experience of the Tao—being in the flow, following The Way. It is the way of the heart, your heart, no longer a forgotten phrase, but a daily experience.

Then you transform:

Limited	⟶	Unlimited
Bound	⟶	Boundless
Ordinary	⟶	Extraordinary
Finite	⟶	Infinite

The more you journey inside, the more you access deeper parts of who you really are—unlimited, unbound, extraordinary, and infinite. Parts of you that have always been there.

•

"Knock and you find you have been inside all the time."

RUMI

•

Be honest. On some level, you know this already. Most people intuitively sense this is true—that at their core they are love. At their essence, they are deeper and bigger than what they experience in daily life. Most people have an experience that life is much more vast, deep, and profound than that which they allow themselves to experience. Living from your core is the answer.

All of this is entirely optional—your heart doesn't force anything. It patiently sits waiting for your visits to whisper its secrets, speak of its love for you, inspire you with compassion. The heart's longing is palpable. You are like a prince born into the basement of a palace.

The palace is your heart. The keys to the door, and every door in the palace, are the keys of meditation. You suspect that on some level the basement isn't really all there is. Maybe you can hear sounds from the banquet hall, music from the orchestra that plays, or smell the magnificent feast that is waiting for you. In whatever way, you intuitively have a sense, no matter how strong or weak that sense is, that there is more to the darkness of the basement. You are royalty born in hiding—waiting for the right call to take over the throne.

Meditation masters live in the palace of the heart.

Once in your heart, you can talk and act from that place. Maybe this will look like your core values come out into the world. Maybe it means you say what you mean more often, or that you say things with deeper conviction. Or that you say less, and the little you say resonates and has the power to move mountains.

Maybe you find your heart is where the secret of life lies—the secret of your life. Maybe your heart, rather than your head, can be an oracle that sets your direction. Maybe you can actually start to feel the desire for all of your words to be from God. Maybe you find that people respond to you differently. Maybe you attract different people into your life, people who sense a quality in you that comes simply from your ability to access your heart. Maybe it's all actually about being more in line with your heart's longing, whatever form that may take.

Maybe you've forgotten what it's like to feel your heart, and even the phrase "find your heart" sounds familiar but is not something you can use. Maybe the last two paragraphs sound as if they were written about someone else. If that's the case then you stand to benefit most from this book. I know. That was exactly the position in which I once found myself.

AN IMPORTANT LESSON

A teacher once gave me feedback: "You do not live from your heart. Do you think I am right?"

I thought about what he said. I knew the word "heart" and I knew the word "live," but honestly I didn't really understand the question. When I told my teacher this he replied, "It's probably a good indication that what I said is true." I still didn't understand what he meant.

"You are so used to living in your head you have totally forgotten what it's like to live from your heart. I may as well have asked you what it's like living on the moon! You may have read about the moon. You may know a lot about the moon. You may have even seen the moon at night. It's not the same as having the experience of living on the moon."

I turned red with embarrassment. Imagine having no idea of the experience of living from my heart at the age of thirty! I was speechless. If I was honest with myself, I had to admit that the teacher's words were true. I went blank as if my mind had been asked a question to which it had no answer.

He gently continued. "The solution is to find the keys to your heart. If you want to, of course."

"So what are the keys to my heart?" I asked, still slightly embarrassed.

"The keys to meditation, of course!"

The more you meditate, the more the qualities of your deepest being flow outward into the world—*so that other people feel the difference.* Have you ever met someone who has a certain kind of presence? Someone whose presence in the room is palpable? In my experience, many teachers with whom I have trained have had this ability that allows the innermost to radiate outwards. I remember listening once to Sogyal Rinpoche (author of *The Tibetan Book of Living and Dying*) when he suddenly stopped his presentation and bowed toward the entrance to the hall. In the doorway was an eighty-year-old Buddhist nun who spoke no English. She walked into the room and smiled. I have never experienced such a force of love flowing from another person. Without any words she radiated the energy of love. I remember my body shaking with tears at the beauty of her presence.

Calm Reminder

To remind us of the ocean of calm that's within us now, change the menu headings on your Blackberry or PDA. Add "Be Calm Now" or "Choose Calm." Every time you use your BlackBerry/PDA it will remind you to practice calm.

We intuitively assess other people all the time—whether we like it or not, whether we know we are doing it or not. In the end, the quality of our center gets to flow into the world so that other people can feel it. Meditation is not just about creating a set of experiences for ourselves, but about having that set of experiences essentially for the benefit of others.

●

"The circumference of the circle has found its Center."

OSHO

●

At the start of this chapter we spoke about transforming:

Chaos   ———⟶   Calm

Noise   ———⟶   Silence

Activity   ———⟶   Stillness

But how can you get from:

$$\text{Effort} \longrightarrow \text{Effortlessness}$$

Fortunately that's the subject for the next section of this book.

PART TWO
The Essentials

In this section you will find the answers to these questions:

How do you transform effort to effortlessness?

●

What are the amazing Eight Laws of Meditation?

●

How can Five Secrets of Super Calm powerfully create
states of calm, bliss, love, delight, and compassion?

●

What are Eleven Powerful Ways to protect the calm you have
(or the Eleven Thieves who threaten your journey)?

●

What is the Wisdom of the Seven Sages
(or the Seven Really Useful Ideas to help your journey)?

3

The Eight Laws of Meditation

In this chapter you will learn eight Laws of Meditation that will
help you create, deepen, and dynamically improve your ability
to move from calm to Super Calm.

LAW NUMBER ONE: RELAX!

In the meditation courses I run for companies, the first thing I tell
executives to do is relax! The journey to your core can only happen
when you relax. Most Super Busy people approach learning new
tasks like a sprinter waiting for the starter's gun in a race—the body
is tense, muscles taut; there is a goal to achieve.

Meditation is the opposite of effort. Meditation is much more
like slipping into a warm luxurious bubble bath—you can feel
the warmth of the water, smell the fragrance of the soaps, hear the
running water. As you slip into the bath the only question is "Mmm-
mmm … how long can I enjoy this?"

The journey to the ocean of calm needs to be easy—
otherwise, if we had to struggle, fight, and battle to get there
we wouldn't be calm when we arrived.

If you find your body becoming tense and tight, remember this law. Take a deep breath and allow the tension in your body to release. In the techniques section of this book, the practices associated with the Path of the Open Body have useful tips to build the feeling of relaxation while learning new tasks.

the power of relaxed alertness

A woman who went to yoga three times a week came to a meditation master and complained, "I don't get it. I've done yoga for years, and I'm trying really hard at meditating but it's not working."

The master replied, "You need relaxed alertness rather than tense and contracted effort. You think you need to 'work hard to learn.'"

Can you remember the time you first learned to giggle? Or the first time your body really shook with laughter? Remember those times. Now, allow a smile to appear, and then start the practice again.

The harder you try, the less you succeed
because the First Golden Law of Meditation is "Relax."

LAW NUMBER TWO: A SENSE OF PLAYFULNESS

To really understand the first law, it is useful to approach your meditation practice with a playful attitude, which is the second law of meditation. Often we remember the things that were a pleasure to learn. Without playfulness we risk making our bodies tense and tight, which moves us in the opposite direction of the first law: Relax! Once you understand this law, the journey to your heart is quicker and easier.

Study a kitten playing with a ball of wool; see how focused and attentive he is. Alert and watchful, yet he knows it is just a game.

He is not striving to be the best ball-playing cat on the block. He is not striving to win the Cat Olympics ball playing competition. His game has the quality of delight and innocence. He can easily be distracted by some other game and then return to playing with the ball of wool, not berating himself for having forgotten to practice. Let your practice have the quality of softness, playfulness, innocence, and delight; not rigidity and hardness.

LAW NUMBER THREE: GENTLENESS

Remember a time you saw a mother holding a newborn child. Remember the exquisite gentleness and tenderness with which she caressed the child? This is the same way you need to treat yourself, with great gentleness and care. Super Busy people have enough rules at which to fail, enough hardness on themselves without creating a new set of rules at which to fail. Understanding this law powerfully moves you through times of frustration when learning how to meditate. It doesn't mean you "don't give a damn" or should be careless.

The Calm Commuter

Take a breath in. Close your eyes. Count to three. Exhale for a count of three. Ensure there is no pause between your in- and out-breath. This circular breathing increases the amount of energy you feel.

LAW NUMBER FOUR: THE OPEN BODY

Imagine your physical body is a hose that carries water. If the hose is kinked and blocked, then less water gets through. In the same way, your physical body carries energy. If your body is blocked and contracted then less energy can be carried. The diagram below shows that when the physical body is tight and unrelaxed, it is difficult to journey to the ocean of calm. Your attention gets caught on the surface, and cannot drop deeper. Your body needs to be relaxed and open.

THE STRESSED BODY

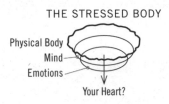

Remember, I said we could go from:

Chaos	⟶	Calm
Noise	⟶	Silence
Activity	⟶	Stillness
Effort	⟶	Effortlessness

The first four laws allow us to relax, be playful, be gentle, and have an open body. We get to be effortless. Effort works in the opposite direction from getting to your core.

But how can you build calm, deepen it, and protect it?

Scanning the Body

Focus on the following muscle groups: • Small muscles around your eyes • Muscles in your forehead

• Your abdomenal muscles

For the next hour, check these muscles to ensure they are

calm and relaxed. The more you relax your physical body, the more calm you have. Relax these muscles—you may want to gently massage around your eyes and forehead. Check these areas every ten minutes for the next hour and ensure they are relaxed. This will enable you to work with less effort.

LAW NUMBER FIVE: BUILD CALM—USE YOUR ATTENTION

To create calm—focus on calm. One of the great Laws of Meditation is that where your attention goes, energy flows.

Let me give you some examples.

If you place your attention on positive thoughts, you get positive-thought energy.

If you place your attention on negative thoughts, you get negative-thought energy.

If you place your attention on a picture of a deity, you get the energy of the deity.

If you place your attention on your heart, you magnify your heart energy.

If you place your attention on your frenetically racing mind, you get "frenetic-mind" energy.

This is something you already know. Great athletes know to keep their attention on positive images of success prior to a match, rather than on negative ones. In your own life, if you want to complete a project you narrow your focus onto that project. This magnifies the work to be done or "energy" of the project. The same is true for calm; the more focus you put on calm, the more calm flows.

Hindu saints place their attention on a mantra to magnify the energy or quality of the sound. For example, the sound "OM" represents a certain aspect of the universe of all things manifested. Buddhist monks may put their attention on the space between their eyebrows, or third eye, to magnify the quality of energy that is there. The Christian saint repeats the word "Jesus" to magnify the quality of his deity. Why? Because what you notice you magnify.

Don't just take my word for it. Try the following exercises.

The Candle Flame

At home, light a candle and place it an arm's distance from your eyes. For five minutes gently keep your eyes focused on the candle flame.

Notice what happens to the outside world when you keep your focus on the flame. Notice the awareness of the sensations in your body. Notice what happens to your concerns about the day.

The outside world and concerns about the day are still there, but not as stressful as before, as your attention magnifies the calm energy of the candle.

The Belly Breath

Take a deep breath from your belly.

With the next breath keep your chest and shoulders still and breathe from your belly.

Now breathe so deeply you can feel the belt of your pants.

Now breathe again and hold the breath for two seconds. Repeat three times.

LAW NUMBER SIX: BUILD CALM—THE LAW OF REPETITION

A top U.S. basketball player joined a leading NBA team, and the coach had him shoot baskets from three feet out, over and over again. The player complained that he already knew how to shoot from this distance and wanted more excitement and challenge. The coach replied, "You keep shooting from three feet out until it's habit, then I'll get you to shoot four feet out until that's habit. Eventually you'll be able to shoot from any point on the court blindfolded."

Meditation requires repeating basic, obvious, and simple steps over and over again.

LAW NUMBER SEVEN: MAINTAIN CALM—THE CHAIN ANALOGY

Meditation is like a chain that leads to your heart—each link in the chain represents a moment of doing the practice. For example, if the technique is placing your attention on your heart, then each link is placing your attention moment by moment on your heart.

THE CHAIN ANALOGY

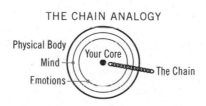

LAW NUMBER EIGHT: FIND CALM EVERYWHERE—HIDDEN GEMS

Meditation is like digging for treasure and throwing away ordinary stones that contain priceless gems inside. Meditation is the revolution of creating the utterly profound from the utterly ordinary, obvious, and everyday. Executives often have a hard time believing that anything profound can come from altering something as simple as breath, or by repeating a certain word, or changing their focus. And yet, the height of enlightenment is experienced by harnessing the most ordinary capacities.

●

"Embarrassment ...
at having overlooked
the obvious for so long"

THE THIRD PATRIARCH OF ZEN,
when asked what emotion he felt upon becoming enlightened

●

The Serene Subway
Close your eyes. Imagine your spine is a tube of pure white light. Imagine the light glows brighter and more intense. The light represents healing and clarity.

SUMMARY OF THE EIGHT LAWS OF MEDITATION
The Eight Laws allow you to transform effort to effortlessness, to power through difficulties with ease, and to multiply the amount of calm in your life. Remember them before starting each meditation.

You Are Effortless	**1** Relax!
	2 Be Playful
	3 Be Gentle
	4 Open Body
You Build Calm	**5** Use Attention to Focus on Calm
You Deepen Calm	**6** Repetition
You Maintain Calm	**7** The Chain Analogy
You Find Calm Everywhere	**8** Hidden Gems

SUPER BUSY: THE UPSIDE

Here's the good news. Busy people use the same skills to create success that the Dalai Lama uses to meditate. That's why busy people are the perfect students to learn meditation. Let me give you some examples.

Successful people have the capacity to focus. One of the most important, if not *the* most important, skills that underpin the greatest meditation practices (*vipassana,* mantra, breath, concentration, and contemplation) is the ability to focus. When the Dalai Lama repeats a mantra, or places his attention on the space between his eyebrows (or third eye), or focuses on his heart, he uses the amazing power of focus.

In the same way, the Super Busy know all about narrowing their focus onto one topic; whether that person is a lawyer preparing for a case or a currency trader focusing on the Reuters screen, the outside world and all distracting issues are ignored. The currency trader blocks out all distractions and secondary priorities—the desire to phone his wife, start planning a family holiday, talk to his friends, read the paper, finish his tax return, talk to his staff. All of these worthy priorities are put aside. It's *exactly* the same skill the Dalai Lama uses.

The only difference is that they focus on different things—the lawyer on his case, the currency trader on the markets, the Dalai Lama on his mantra, third eye, and heart. All can keep their attention tightly focused *regardless of distractions.*

So powerful is the capacity to focus that if there is only one thing you learn from this book, let it be the awesome power of mastering your attention.

Successful people can do two things at once. Most of us can talk on the phone and check our email. We can "split" our attention. We can drive a car and mentally run through lists of tasks for today. Nearly all of us can walk down the street and be totally lost in stressful thoughts. We can be talking to someone, listening to that person's conversation, and be focusing on our own train of thoughts. This capacity to split our attention on two things at once can be used to profound ends.

The Dalai Lama and all great masters keep part of their attention on their center. For example, you can walk down the street and have part of your attention on the ocean of calm rather than stressful thoughts. You can talk on your cell and have part of your attention on your heart, and so build up the quality of heart energy. You can check your PDA and have part of your attention on mastering your breathing as a way to still the mind.

Attention is lightning fast, automatic, and instant; it all depends on what you use it for.

Successful people overcome challenges. Successful people thrive and grow through challenge, making them perfect candidates for mastering meditation.

Meditation masters are masters because they overcome the obstacles and challenges in meditation in spite of distracting thoughts, or feelings of frustration. Meditation masters recognize that these obstacles will not master them. Great meditators are those who stick to the practice regardless of the challenges and hurdles they face.

●

"There is no enlightenment outside of daily life."
THICH NHAT HANH

●

Successful people master subtlety. At peak performance, superior athletes understand the critical importance of subtlety. Let me give you an example. The Swedish Winter Olympic team returned home with zero medals from the 1998 Winter Olympics. They calculated that if they had improved their performances by 5 percent they would have won the majority of the medals. Small changes make big results.

Meditation masters are obsessed with subtle movements. They focus their attention on subtle shifts in their breath to see how present they are. They are obsessed with small shifts in body posture as an indicator of how present they are.

zen story

After one year in a monastery, a Zen monk complained, "All I have learned about is breathing." After five years in the monastery, the monk complained, "All I have learned is breathing." When he reached enlightenment the elderly monk smiled and said, "Finally, I have learned about breathing."

Successful people know about training. In business, knowledge is power. To maintain their edge, successful people are keen to improve their skills via courses, executive coaches, and learning from role models. The Dalai Lama and all spiritual masters realize that, just like learning to play tennis, golf, or any sport, the quickest way to improve is through training. Training is a key part of all major spiritual disciplines.

YOU HAVE ALL IT TAKES TO SUCCEED

The most profound meditators share a similar skill set to the Super Busy.

Ability to focus. One of the crucial skills is harnessing and controlling your power of focus.

Can do two things at once. This means you can have part of your attention on your heart while doing mundane activities like walking down the street, commuting, and talking with others.

Can overcome obstacles. Great meditators, like successful business people, have great perseverance to complete their tasks regardless of distractions.

Can master subtlety. Attention to the small details differentiates masters from apprentices.

Know the value of training. Just as when learning a sport, finding great teachers/coaches is important.

The Five Secrets of Super Calm

For thousands of years ancient meditation secrets have been passed down from meditation master to student. The secrets enable the student to create more calm and access more joy, bliss, love, and compassion. From the Himalayan monasteries, Tibetan temples, and Indian shrines, I reveal five of the most important secrets.

SECRET NUMBER ONE: DEALING WITH DISTRACTIONS

"I just can't meditate! I have too many thoughts!"

We've all been there. This is the most common struggle with meditation. Here is the ancient secret used by meditation masters.

There are two options for dealing with distractions. Look at the following two timelines. Each link in the chain represents a unit of time in meditation practice.

OPTION 1

More frustration
Inner Dialogue about frustration
Frustration
Aware of distraction
Distracted
Focused

OPTION 2

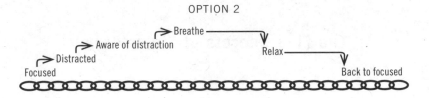

Breathe, relax, and return your focus. The second option quickly returns the meditator to building calm.

SECRET NUMBER TWO: THE LONGER, THE BETTER

The benefits of *Meditation in a New York Minute* build and develop over time.

"How did Tiger Woods get so good?"

We all know the answer—practice.

Tiger Woods didn't get to be good overnight. Practice—and remember—have fun, be gentle, relax, and breathe. Start by meditating whenever you have a few moments to spare. As you'll see in the techniques section, almost any activity can be an invitation to deeper awareness—commuting, walking down the street, working out at the gym, even taking a shower. If you seize every opportunity to practice these techniques, you'll soon find that your effort will result in a cumulative total of an hour a day spent in meditation, which is exactly the result we're aiming for. Your persistence is the key.

Many years ago my father taught me the "Analogy of the Garden Tap." He was trying to describe how often when we pray there doesn't seem to be any benefit. When you first meditate, nothing seems to happen. You are like a rusty garden tap that hasn't been used for years. Years of neglect have blocked the tap. When you turn the tap on, nothing happens. With gradual persistence, the first few drops emerge—a discolored brown. With persistence the first trickle of water appears. Eventually, with practice, pure clear water flows freely from the tap. The key is persistence. I've often remembered my father's analogy.

SECRET NUMBER THREE:
SUPER CALM REQUIRES A PORTFOLIO OF TECHNIQUES

How do you learn to play the piano? You begin by playing one note. Then two. Then by putting together combinations of notes. Each technique in this book is like learning one note on the piano. The goal is to have so many notes that the most beautiful relaxing melody can be played. With practice, your life becomes the symphony of love, the music of the divine, the song of joy, an ode not to life but of Life.

The aim is to find many notes, a symphony of techniques, to allow you to meditate throughout the day.

SECRET NUMBER FOUR: NOTHING FAILS LIKE SUCCESS

There are no such concepts as "succeeding" or "failing" in meditation; there is simply doing the practice. Concepts like "success" and "failure" automatically imply you will be unable to meet the First Law of Meditation: Relax! Nor will you be gentle or have a sense of playfulness. Most people, if they know they can fail, don't immediately find a great release and sense of relief flooding through their systems. Their muscles don't instantly soften, and tension from the day doesn't melt away. Their breath doesn't relax and allow their breathing to become deep and full, creating a sense of calm in the mind. In fact, just the opposite occurs!

Superior meditators intimately understand the principals of relax, be gentle, playful, and create an open body.

The benefit in understanding this secret is that you journey to the ocean of calm more quickly.

SECRET NUMBER FIVE: FIND A TEACHER

Books only go so far. Do what other successful people do—find an executive coach or a meditation coach. Someone to guide you on the way.

REMEMBER THE FIVE SECRETS OF SUPER CALM

Secret One: Effectively deal with distractions. Breathe, relax, and refocus.

Secret Two: The longer, the better. The goal is to swim in the ocean of calm for an hour a day.

Secret Three: Super Calm requires a portfolio of techniques. The more techniques you master the more you swim in the ocean of calm.

Secret Four: Nothing fails like success. The journey is the destination!

Secret Five: Find a teacher. To get good, get training!

5

The Eleven Thieves

COMMON TRAPS AND HOW TO AVOID THEM

On the journey to the ocean of calm there are a number of thieves lurking in the dark whose only intent is to steal your treasure, to prevent you from reaching your core. Their intent is to ambush you. Some of the thieves work by leading you off the path and into frustrating dead ends. Others disguise themselves as friends only to prevent you from going deeper in your journey. They hope to remain hidden.

Here I expose them, so you can recognize them. You will be able to access even deeper parts of your core when you understand this section. For each problem you now have a solution. During my years of meditation practice, I have been led onto numerous dead-end paths. Often painful misconceptions and erroneous beliefs increased the amount of mental anguish and stress I experienced. What follows is a list of the most ruthless thieves, how they operate, and how to avoid them. I wish I had possessed this list when I first tried meditation. The list includes the most common pitfalls in the journey to create calm.

Often, these thieves will remain hidden during brief practices. But, as you begin to practice meditation for longer periods, they will inevitably make an appearance. That's why it's so important to be able to recognize them when they arrive.

THIEF ONE: THE ONE-THOUSAND THOUGHTS

"Help! When I meditate I have a thousand thoughts running through my head."

This is the most common experience for meditators. The solution is to get into your body. Do some brief physical exercise to enliven your body prior to your practice. This can range from simply rolling your shoulders and stretching to vigorously shaking your hands or running on the spot. This will help calm your mind.

•

"Come to your senses. Lose your Mind."

BRAD BLANTON

•

The other solution is to keep holding the chain—each moment—refocusing on the sensations in the body and experiences in the outside world. Thoughts will always be there; it is simply a matter of

1 Allowing them to be there, and

2 Refocusing on your practice.

The analogy is that thoughts are like cars racing by on a freeway. When you first start to meditate there are hundreds of cars racing by so quickly. There seems no way to stop them. You can't chase after each of them. You simply observe them; let them be. After a while, by simply letting them be and observing them, the traffic starts to slow. Fewer and fewer cars appear. Eventually, only a few cars appear.

Then your thoughts appear like cars on a main road—still cars, but traveling slower. Eventually your thoughts appear like cars on a quiet country road—appearing in the distance, in the background. Slowly, even fewer cars appear until you are by a beautiful tranquil river in the countryside smelling the roses for the first time.

What do you do when thoughts arise? Remember the First Secret of Calm—breathe, relax, and get focused!

THIEF TWO: THE STORM OF EMOTIONS

"My emotions are going through the roof. What can I do?"

Given our hectic lifestyles, it's natural and normal for us to experience intense emotions. Often when we become still, we become more aware of the emotions within us. These often prevent us from experiencing calm, which is deeper than both thoughts and feelings. The solution is not to block out, resist, or try to avoid intense emotions. The answer is to go through them. There are two solutions to this.

1 The total awareness technique is perfect for it, or

2 Use the body to express, however slightly, the emotions you are having. For example, shake your wrists to remove tension from your body. Jog on the spot for a few moments. Put on loud music and dance. Use your time at the gym to release the emotional charge of the day.

THIEF THREE: MONKEY MIND

"I am constantly distracted. Issues run through my head and call my attention."

The answer is to keep a pen and notepad handy. Write down a list of your concerns as each item appears. In this way, they get dealt with and no longer visit you to distract you.

THIEF FOUR: THE FALSE MASTER

Super Calm meditation techniques require mastery of the most basic, simple, and obvious of human capacities—for example, your breath, focus, intention, your body, inner dialogue, and imagination. The biggest trap is for busy executives to conclude, "I've mastered it."

Saying, "Meditation: that's just breathing," is like saying, "Astronomy: that's just twinkle twinkle little star." While this is true to some extent, it ignores the art, the subtlety, of perfecting your breath. The solution is to understand this thief—recognize the thought, "Oh, I've mastered this," as being a trap. Then return to the practice.

simple, but not easy

The banker practiced a few breaths at his desk.

The practice was from the Path of the 13,000 Steps—to breathe deeply from the belly no matter what, but to keep breathing.

I'll repeat that line—in case you are skim reading—"to breathe deeply from the belly no matter what, but to keep breathing."

He was getting some benefit, but not much. I could tell he was thinking something along the lines of, "I'm a senior executive in a global bank, I have a staff of thirty reporting directly to me, I manage close to a billion dollars in equity every day, and some executive coach has offered to revolutionize my life, and all he is doing is teaching me how to breathe?!"

I know that's what I'd be thinking if I were in his position.

I shouted loudly and abruptly, "Aaaagh!"

The startled banker opened his eyes and said, "What? Are you OK?"

"What's happening to your breathing?" I asked in a calm voice.

He saw that I was OK and checked his breathing.

"Well it stopped," he said, still out of breath from the cry.

"But I told you to practice no matter what," I reminded him.

"Well I wanted to know what had happened," he retorted, starting to get annoyed.

"What's happening to your breathing now?" I asked again.

The banker huffed a bit, and then reluctantly said, "It's a bit shallow."

"But I told you to breathe deeply no matter what," I pointed out quietly.

"But I'm talking."

"Can't you breathe deeply while you talk?"

"Well, of course," he replied, more annoyed.

"And what's happening to your breathing now?" I asked gently.

After checking for a while he replied, "Well it's shallow, but that's only because I'm starting to get frustrated."

"But I told you to practice no matter what," I repeated. "You see, anyone can sit in a chair, close his eyes, and breathe. That's like kindergarten level. The challenge and art of this technique is to do it no matter what emotional state you are in. In this situation a shout, the feeling of surprise, talking, and the feeling of anger—each of them were able to throw you from your practice. Instantly."

He started to see the point.

"This is one of the hardest practices I know, because it seems so simple. Being able to take a deep breath is like being able to hold a tennis racket for the first time. It doesn't mean you can hit the ball yet, let alone play forehand, backhand, lob, volley, smash, and serve. This will take you about fifteen years to master."

So the technique is not just to breathe deeply, but to breathe deeply in different situations.

THIEF FIVE: FALSE EXPECTATIONS

Often people expect to create calm every moment, in every situation, at the first attempt. Remember my father's analogy of the rusty garden tap—sometimes it takes time for pure, clear water to unblock years of disuse.

THIEF SIX: THE JUDGE

The number one problem people encounter is the inner critic—or the judge. You can recognize the judge by the questions:

What should I be feeling?

Is this right?

Should I be feeling this?

What are other people experiencing, and why aren't I?

These are all normal questions, and the key is to not be distracted. Keep bringing your attention back to sensations in your body.

The strongest message I've heard many meditation teachers repeat is, "All is well! Whatever you experience is fine." Remember a sense of playfulness.

a dream of failure

I had a dream that I was teaching a managing director, called John, meditation. He did not look happy.

He had practiced meditation for a week, and things had not gone well.

"What's been happening?" I asked.

His shoulders were hunched slightly. He felt embarrassed because he had not continued with the practice. Depression, sadness, feeling down, or feeling guilty are not emotions that meditation should be creating. More like joy, bliss, connectedness, a sense of well-being, and calm.

"Every time I start the practice I get, you know, distracted," he explained.

"Believe me, I do know," I replied, as this is one of the most common challenges meditators face.

Rather than stress the benefits of meditation, I decided on a different approach.

"John," I had a serious look on my face, "We've worked together for two sessions now, and, with your specific personality, your skills and attributes, your characteristics, I believe that you will ... " I pause for emphasis.

" ... consistently fail at meditation."

In the dream, John's eyes widened in surprise.

He stopped breathing at this point and looked slightly shocked.

I looked at him

He looked at me.

"Then again," I continued "that's exactly what happens to me everyday. So, I give you complete permission to fail. I'll even write you a note," I joked.

"What do you mean?" said John.

"Every meditator's attention wanders. Zen masters who have practiced for many years have wandering attention from time to time. The key is to know what to do with 'wandering.' Either we get stressed and depressed like you have. Or we simply choose to repeat the practice, moment by moment. If your attention wanders, just return to the practice, without judging. So just relax and enjoy it. You will be less stressed, have more fun, and you will get to your core quicker."

THIEF SEVEN: CALM = HAVING NO THOUGHTS

I spent many painful years expecting that the goal of meditation was to allow the mind to become still. A still mind, for me, meant zero thoughts.

This of course led to disillusionment, frustration, and disappointment, as no matter how hard I tried, I kept having thoughts. Almost regardless of how serene the location, or how profound the teacher, or how successful the technique, I kept having thoughts!

Solution: As long as you are in a body, you will have thoughts. All the sages and masters have thoughts. Even the ones preaching "no mind" spirituality have thoughts! You can no more stop your thoughts than you can stop the wind from blowing. It's not about having thoughts; it's about not attaching to them when they appear. It's about totally allowing and accepting thoughts when they arise, *and* not putting your attention (focus) on them. During meditation, your attention and focus is always on your meditation practice.

THIEF EIGHT: CALM = HAVING LESS THOUGHTS

This is similar to the trap above. You have sixty thousand thoughts a day; that's a lot of counting. If you are counting thoughts, you are placing your attention on them and not on the practice.

Solution: Keep your attention on whatever meditation practice you are doing and don't bother about the thoughts that arise. For most of our life we are conditioned to watch, chase, analyze, compare, and evaluate thoughts when they arise. Meditation is the discipline of detaching your attention from this activity and focusing on your specific practice.

THIEF NINE: CALM = HAVING ONLY POSITIVE THOUGHTS

This is another variation on the last two.

Again this is difficult to do, given our habitual obsession on our thoughts. If you remember the diagram defining meditation on page 54, it is a journey to a place deeper than your thoughts—regardless of their content. Perhaps, for the first time in your life you get to ignore your thoughts. (You don't push them away or argue with them when they arise, but you simply and totally accept them and place your attention elsewhere.) Your mind is like a continuously and endlessly blabbing relative who talks incessantly. Previously you may have believed these thoughts were vital to your existence. So you listened obsessively to the blabbing.

You get to ignore the blabbing because your interest is now in the core of your being, a place deeper than thoughts, deeper than feeling. Therefore you ignore them—you don't shoot the blabbing relative or enter into a discourse with him. Allow the thoughts to be there and place your attention elsewhere.

In meditation you get to focus on a path that takes you deeper than the thoughts—regardless of their content, as I said. Regardless of whether they are positive, negative, or neutral. Regardless of whether they are profound or mundane. All thoughts are let go.

THIEF TEN: A GOOD MEDITATOR *NEVER* ATTACHES TO THOUGHTS

When I first learned meditation, I thought this was the key. It's a painful trap. My thirst for being at my core meant I went to extreme lengths to achieve this. For example, I rationalized that if my core is deeper than thoughts, then never listen to them. Or, if living in the present is never grabbing onto thoughts, then never grab onto thoughts.

This is useful if you live in solitary confinement in a Himalayan monastery with no tasks or activities to carry out. However, the rest of us need to use the mind as a tool. We pick it up when we need it and drop it when it is not needed. But at the moment, many of us are used by our minds, rather than the other way around.

THIEF ELEVEN: MIND IS THE ENEMY OF CALM

There are no enemies in meditation! Neither distractions, thoughts, interruptions, nor feelings. There is simply returning to the practice.

●

"It's hard to have enemies.
Especially when they have outposts inside your head."

SALLY KEMPTON

●

After meditation, the mind is again picked up, like a tool to be used. If the mind is like a Ferrari racing car, meditation is not destroying the car. Rather, meditation is knowing how to slow the car, leave it when necessary, and start again when it is useful. Great meditators know when to use their minds and when to drop their minds.

SUMMARY: THE ELEVEN THIEVES AND HOW TO AVOID THEM

Challenge	Solutions
One Thousand Thoughts	• Allow them to be there.
	• Keep refocusing on your practice.
Storm of Emotions	• Total awareness technique is perfect for this (see page 96).
	• Use your body to express, however slightly, your emotions.
Monkey Mind	• Write down your list of "to do's" as each appears.

Challenge	Solutions
False Master	• Recognize that the thought, "I've mastered this," is a trap. Then, return to the practice.
	• Mastery is doing the technique constantly.
False Expectations	• Remember the analogy of the rusty garden tap; often it takes time for pure, clear water to flow.
The Judge	• Keep bringing your attention back to sensations in your body, and remember the first three Laws of Meditation—relax, be gentle, and be playful.
Super Calm = No Thoughts	• You will always have thoughts. Allow them to be there. Simply keep your attention on your meditation practice regardless of what thoughts appear.
Super Calm = Less Thoughts	• Totally allow thoughts to be there, like a distant sound, or an image appearing in your peripheral vision. Gently keep your attention on your practice.

Challenge	Solutions
Super Calm = Positive Thoughts	• Meditation is a journey deeper than thoughts regardless of what thoughts they are (positive, negative, profound, mundane). Allow them to be there. Gently keep your attention on your practice.
"I'll Never Use My Mind Again!"	• The mind is like a tool. Use it when you need it. Drop it when you don't. Great meditators know the difference.
"I Must Ignore My Thoughts"	• Meditation has nothing to do with thoughts. It has everything to do with focusing on the now.
	• Meditation is like holding onto a chain—pulling link-by-link, moment-by-moment, into the core.

In the storm of thoughts only one thing remains—placing your attention on the meditation as if it were the only thing to pull you through.

6

Seven Sages for Your Journey

To help you on your journey, imagine seven wise old sages who have been around since the beginning of time. Each approaches you and whispers in your ear, "Your journey starts here. I have a really good idea that I have taught every saint, sage, and swami since the beginning of time. I hope you find it useful."

1. START SMALL

Always start with one technique rather than trying to master many. Choose one technique and practice it for thirty days. If you find the technique has not worked, then move on to another. Learning many different techniques at the same time can be confusing.

2. PRACTICE AT HOME

Often it's easier to practice at home to build confidence. Sit in a quiet location and spend thirty minutes reading and practicing the technique.

It's useful to have this book close by for ease of reference.

3. THE TEN MINUTE RULE

Spend ten minutes reading the technique in full including the tips, common problems, FAQs, and background. Your journey will be quicker and more rewarding.

4. DO NOT SKIM READ THE INSTRUCTIONS

Read each instruction slowly—what transforms your breath and your attention is incredibly subtle.

5. START EASY, PROGESS GRADUALLY

The first time you play tennis, you don't step onto center court at Wimbledon. If a practice can be done in different situations, then start at home and progressively build the degree of difficulty. For example, with the body awareness technique on page 93, start at home, and then try it while walking down the street. Then try it on the subway, then at the gym, and so on, each time gradually building the types of situations in which you try the technique.

6. BE PRACTICAL AND SAFE

In all things be practical. If a technique is proving difficult to master and is increasing your level of frustration, then remember the first four Laws of Meditation (relax, be playful, be gentle, and create an open body). Then see if another technique might be more useful. Similarly, the techniques are meant to support you in your daily life, not to threaten it. If a technique makes you tired or drowsy when you are at work, then stop doing it, take a few deep breaths, and maybe take a walk around the block if your work situation allows.

If your practices are causing you to lose focus at work, then stop them, re-read the guidelines, and start again at home.

Be aware of your surroundings and of others. Always be aware of your own physical safety and that of those around you.

7. PRACTICE WITH OTHERS

Reading a book is great—but rarely enough. There are many teachers of meditation. The benefits multiply when you do it with others. "When one or more are gathered in my name, I am there also."

SUMMARY OF THE SEVEN SAGES

Start small.

Practice at home.

Remember the Ten Minute Rule.

Read the instructions slowly.

Start easy, progress gradually.

Be practical and safe.

Practice with others.

7

Take Time for Calm

I want to let you in on a secret. The truth is, you have already mastered the keys to meditation. The techniques in this book may be new to you, but the basic skills used in meditation are the same ones you use every day, in all the situations of daily life. Here's a story to illustrate:

the lawyer and the holy man

"Meditation? Me? I can never sit still. I am the most unlikely person to ever be calm."

The speaker was a lawyer from a large firm expressing his view of relaxing effortlessly.

"I'm just too busy. I tried relaxation techniques in the past. I could never do it," he continued.

I understood his position. We all live such busy lives that learning meditation seems just another chore or burden. Often we think only "spiritual" or "holy" people can meditate. Or that the skills needed to meditate are for saints sitting on mountaintops.

"In your job," I replied, "I imagine you have to focus to get the job done?"

"Of course," the lawyer said.

"Let me ask you: Do you have the capacity to breathe?"

"Yes."

"You clearly have the ability to make sounds, as I can hear you respond to my questions."

"Yes," he replied as his eyes were glazing over with boredom.

"Do you have the ability to have a clear intention?"

"Yes."

"Can you remember a scene from the last movie you watched?"

"Yes," the banker repeated, glancing at his watch.

"There you have it! Congratulations. You have all the skills that the Dalai Lama uses whenever he meditates."

The lawyer frowned and looked at me suspiciously.

I smiled and continued. "You have keys which underpin the major meditation techniques in Eastern religions. When Maharishi Mahesh Yogi, one of the most profound teachers on the planet, sits down to meditate, he uses these keys. When Zen masters meditate, they use the same skills you have. The First Patriarch of Zen used them. So do Christian saints, Buddhist monks, Sufi mystics, and Tantric masters. All of them use exactly the same keys you have—the ability to focus, to control breathing, to make sounds (such as mantras), to use imagination (or visualization). Well done!" I said as I became genuinely excited by the message that anyone can meditate.

The lawyer seemed surprised. "Are you saying I have the same keys the Dalai Lama uses?"

"Absolutely. The Dalai Lama, when he sits to meditate, uses these keys. You have everything inside you, now, to make your journey to the ocean of calm. The deepest, most profound meditation experience that has ever occurred on the planet occurred because of these keys. What is exceptional about the Dalai Lama is his ability to use the keys. Most of all he has the ability to hold onto the chain of meditation regardless of the obstacles. The rest then is up to grace."

"So how can I have such profound experiences?" asked the lawyer.

"All the keys are free, you use them all the time, you've had them since birth. You just need some training on how to use the keys; that's all."

Most people believe meditation requires special skills. It does not. Meditation is fueled by the most common, ordinary, and intensely human capacities. A meditation master is someone who has mastered each of these keys, in different situations. Let me explain. Previously, walking down the street was a time for you to worry more. Now you have techniques to place your attention on the ocean of calm. Previously, your commute was used to increase *stress* by placing your attention on your frenetic mind. Now you can increase *calm* by using the techniques to place attention on accessing the ocean of calm. Here's an example.

The boss of the world's third largest pension fund is busy. In fact, he is Super Busy. During an executive coaching session he said, "Impossible. I have enough trouble trying to meet all my existing deadlines. I can't find an hour a day to create calm."

"Let's look," I replied. Here's the exercise I gave him.

CREATING CALM FOR ONE HOUR A DAY: AN EXERCISE

In the third section of this book, you'll learn techniques to practice throughout the day—while commuting, taking a shower, even working out at the gym. By completing the following exercise, you'll get a better idea of just how many opportunities for meditation await you, without changing your busy schedule at all!

SELF-ASSESSMENT QUIZ

A Identify the amount of time you spend traveling to work each day.

Subway   _____

Car   _____

Walking   _____

Total number of minutes   _____

B Identify the amount of time spent showering.

Total number of minutes   _____

C Identify the amount of time you spend eating each day.

Total number of minutes   _____

D Identify the amount of time you spend walking each day.

To get your lunch   _____

To the gym/health club   _____

Traveling to meetings   _____

In your office building   _____

Total number of minutes   _____

E Add to the above figure the average number of minutes per day you spend at the gym/health club.

Total number of minutes   _____

The total of A + B + C + D + E = Total number of minutes a day you can spend creating Super Calm. Each of the above situations can potentially be transformed into profound ways to create calm.

Add the combined figures of A + B + C + D + E.

Grand total   _____

Multiply the above figure by five for the number of minutes per workweek. Multiply that by four for the monthly total.

And this excludes weekends! But that's not all!

F For the really advanced, identify the time you spend interacting with people each day.

At work: Staff	_____
Boss	_____
Clients	_____
Colleagues	_____
At home: Family	_____
Other: Friends	_____
Total time spent with people	_____

Each encounter with other people is also an opportunity to practice meditations found in the techniques section of this book. As you can see, the opportunities for practice are almost limitless! You might object:

- "But I need those hours on the subway to do extra work/send emails from my laptop/read on the train."
- "But I get all the relaxation I need just by working out at the gym."
- "I work out the stress from the day by going for a run."
- "I need my commute to catch up on my work."
- "This is vital time for me to really relax."

Of course! These are all valid reasons. Turn to the quiz on pages 22 and 23 and see if you have any of the symptoms of excess stress. If you do, then your time at the gym, running, or yoga is helping, but there's room for improvement.

If I'm in a mischievous mood, I ask participants in my meditation seminars to notice if their buttocks are clenched. One hundred percent at first say, "No!" Then I get them to take a deep breath, gently rock their bodies from side to side on the chair, loosen their abdominal muscles, and check again. One hundred percent of the time the response is, "Oh yeah, I was clenching!" So what's a clench here and there? Nothing. It's just one muscle group. But a single clench combined with clenches in other major muscle groups as the default setting for your body is as unhealthy as it is unnecessary. You can bet your last dollar that if you are clenching your buttocks muscles, you are clenching a whole range of other muscles.

Why would you do it? You don't … I pause for effect … enjoy it, do you?

What possible reason is there for tightening your sphincter muscle while having a conversation? It seems crazy, because it is! Tantric saints refer to the body as being a system of energy—more energy flows when the body is open and relaxed. Common sense tells us that we are expending and tying up energy in our systems that could be used for other purposes.

zen story

A wandering sage knocked on the door of a temple and asked for shelter from the cold. A monk opened the door, saw the sage dressed like a beggar, and told him that the temple was closed. That evening, the monk walked into town and found the sage sitting by the road worshipping a milestone.

"What are you doing? You foolish man! This is just a rock. Why do you worship this?"

The sage looked up and replied, "Your Buddha is in the temple. My Buddha is everywhere. Your temple is made of stone. My temple is my heart. Being one, my Buddha is in all."

The monk bowed down at the feet of the sage.

PART THREE

The Techniques

In this section you will learn:

Nineteen powerful tools to create calm effortlessly

●

What may be the right path for you

●

How to put it all together: The Ideal Day

ABOUT THE TECHNIQUES

The techniques in this book are grouped into different pathways, or different ways to access the core. Each path represents a cluster of similar techniques. This allows you to easily focus on techniques that really work for you. For example, if a breath meditation is particularly useful, you have other breath techniques at your fingertips.

No one path is better than another. It is simply a matter of choosing a path that perfectly suits you, your situation in life, the challenges you face, the specific structure of your day, and that makes your heart sing.

This section will help you locate the path that is most suitable for you.

DIFFERENT PATHS—ONE DESTINATION

Path of 13,000 Steps
Path of Present
Path of Focus
Open Body Path
Your Heart
Path of Remembering
Path of Visualization
Path of Heart

8

The Path of 13,000 Steps

Thirteen thousand is the approximate number of breaths you take each day while you are awake.

This is a collection of tools that focus on changing the usual way we breathe. The phenomenal power of breath meditation is that it can quickly and powerfully bring you closer to the ocean of calm.

When teaching meditation to the coach of the Swedish Winter Olympic Team, Runne Gustafson, I found there were similarities with his training of cross-country skiers. Runne taught the skiers to change the shape of their breathing by breathing from their abdomens. He found this improved their performances through:

- Lowering the heart rate and respiratory rate
- Reducing blood pressure
- Re-oxygenating the system, making it feel more vital and alive
- Lowering the speed at which the brain operates

The techniques in this chapter are:

- Power Breath
- Breathing Energy
- Breath of Life
- Chi Gung Breath for Calm

TECHNIQUE ONE: POWER BREATH

Background

Breath meditations are a key part of the major Eastern spiritual traditions. This technique is from the Tantric tradition, which emphasizes physical sensations to slow the mind and build energy. Tantra is one of the few spiritual approaches that harnesses the five senses in the search for the Divine, rather than suppressing them. In our sensory rich environment, and especially for meditations involving movement and traveling to and from work, Tantra provides a rich tradition for using the senses to create calm anytime/anywhere.

Benefits

- Reduces stress
- Energizes the system
- Can be used anywhere
- Significant benefits in less than a minute
- Great for lowering stress before presentations, during meetings, and when meeting people

Technique

Before you begin, you need to expand your notion of how deep your breathing can be.

Your breath can be divided into four sections:

- Upper chest
- Lower chest
- Upper belly
- Lower belly

Your breath tightens and contracts when you are stressed. This exercise develops your capacity to breathe from the lower belly first, then the upper belly. The suggestion is to do this practice at home and then use it elsewhere as required. There are four stages to this technique.

- Stage 1: Relax all the stomach muscles and take a deep breath into the lowest part of your belly. Keep the upper chest and lower chest still.

- Stage 2: Place your hand beneath your navel. Breathe so your hand moves first.

- Stage 3: Gently and easily allow your stomach muscles to naturally expand your belly so it becomes round and full. Loosen your belt/pants to allow this.

- Stage 4: Let the lower belly fill first and then allow the upper belly to fill with air. Again, keep the upper chest and lower chest as still as possible … any movement in the upper chest should be slight and only after the lower and upper belly have been completely filled with air.

The aim is for each in-breath to reach this same amount of exaggerated expansion. The breathing is being done correctly when you can almost feel the in-breath move your genitals.

Repeat this relaxed and deep breathing ten times.

Tips

- Remain easy, soft, and relaxed in your approach! Effort and contraction and tension are not required for this practice.

- Our habits tend to be deeply ingrained in breathing shallowly. It is extremely easy for meditators to do this a few times then revert to their habitual breathing. Notice any rise and fall in the upper/lower chest to guide your attention back to expanding the lower belly first.

How this works:

In order for your system to experience stress, your physical body needs to contract in specific ways, which causes specific emotions. For example, anger and fear nearly always require your stomach muscles to tighten and contract. By keeping your breathing in a deep and relaxed manner the same emotions are experienced very differently—they seem to have a lower intensity and pass quicker. As soon as you start to feel stress, the power breath can increase your feeling of calm.

Noticing what happens to your breath is a key to understanding what's happening in your emotional world as well. In my experience, I noticed that my breathing stopped when I wanted to hold onto or push away certain situations. My breath became a barometer for the emotional states I wanted to avoid and those I wanted to last longer.

The power breath is extremely useful in increasing your energy, as you continue to breathe in stressful situations.

Some specifics:

• Attention is narrowed to the breath. This reduces your focus on stressful thoughts.

• Slower breathing physiologically slows your mental activity. Slow your breath, slow your mind.

• Relaxing stomach muscles results in stressful situations being experienced in a more relaxed manner.

• Deep breathing increases the amount of oxygen in the bloodstream, which increases your feeling of energy.

Note: I use this technique before every business meeting to quickly reduce/manage stress. It allows my voice to come from a deeper, more powerful place, and my system feels more energetically alive and grounded.

Common Problems

- "I can't pay attention to my breathing *and* focus on what's happening during a meeting."

  For meetings/presentations this technique is best practiced before you begin, as this reduces pre presentation stress. During the meeting/presentation the practice can be dropped and the mind can focus on the content of what's happening. The benefits of the meditation can be achieved from one or two simple breaths and can be used whenever you need to become grounded. With all techniques, use them as long as they are practical and useful.

- "Won't I be embarrassed with my stomach protruding so far out?"

  Despite our cultural addiction to the aesthetics of a flat washboard stomach, most people don't notice this.

"A newborn baby breathes from its belly.
A sage also breathes from his belly.
Only modern man does not."
RAMESH S. BALSAKAR

"He who controls his breath,
controls the universe."
ANONYMOUS

TECHNIQUE TWO: BREATHING ENERGY

Background

There are many Eastern calm practices that use breath and *mantras* (the repetition of a sacred word or syllable) as key techniques. I was told a story about a Russian mystic who first taught this practice. Followers were amazed at the quality of love that emanated from him. When asked why love seemed to flow from him, he described this incredibly simple practice. He taught them a prayer, called the "Jesus Prayer." It involved reciting the name of his God as often as he could.

Benefits

• Easy to do
• Can be done anywhere
• Benefits can be achieved in less than a minute
• Floods the system with the qualities and attributes of the Divine
• Quickly increases the amount of practice done every day

Technique

• Choose a quality (peace, light, love, calm, joy, laughter) or the name of a divinity/entity (God, Jesus, Shiva, Buddha ...).
• With each in-breath whisper out loud the first syllable/phrase of the quality/name. For example:

In-breath	Out-breath
Pure	Love
White	Light
Radiant	Peace
Laugh	ter
Perfect	Calm

In-breath	Out-breath
Je	sus
Shi	va
Budd	ha

Whisper the first part/syllable so that it lasts the full length of the in-breath. If your in breath is four seconds, then the first syllable should take four seconds.

With each out-breath whisper out loud the second syllable of the quality/name. Again, the last part/syllable should last the full length of the out-breath. Your in-breath and out-breath should now sound like "Puuuuuuurrrre Loooooovvvvveeeee."

Now with each in-breath say the first syllable internally. With each out-breath say the last syllable internally. The rise and fall of your breathing are now linked to constant repetition of the quality or divinity you wish to magnify in your life.

Tips
- Slow the breathing down.
- Start the practice in a quiet place at home until it becomes natural and easy for you. As the habit becomes easier, practice it on the way to work, whenever there is an available moment.
- A few simple breaths like this can instantly create a sense of the quality you are repeating.

Common Problems
- "Moving about in the world, especially on trains, has many distractions ... I am constantly pulled away from the repetition."

Build the practice up from different stages to reinforce the habit.

Beginner: Whisper out loud in a quiet place, such as at home, for two minutes. Then say the names internally for two minutes.

Intermediate: Continue the practice, walking around in a relatively quiet place where it is easy to focus on the repetition *and* be safely aware of the world around you. This will assist you in building up the habit of including movement in the meditation while maintaining focus.

Advanced: Continue the practice, walking around in a busy/ crowded place, which requires more trained focus.

Very Advanced: Continue the practice while talking to others.

- "I get anxious if I miss repeating the name."

The simple practice requires creating a new habit, which takes time. Gently, easily, and tenderly bring your attention back to the repetition. Do not judge yourself if your attention wanders ... the last thing busy people want is another list of rules by which they can "fail"! The key is being gentle and nonjudgmental with yourself.

TECHNIQUE THREE: BREATH OF LIFE

Background

This technique is an ancient meditation from the Vigyan Bhairava and Sochanda Tantra written approximately four thousand years ago. The meditation is one of 112 practices given by Shiva to his consort Devi who asked the deity for instructions on spiritual practice.

Benefits

- Slows the mind
- Reduces stress

- A short amount of practice can produce benefits

Technique

Sit in a quiet place.

Notice the breath as it gently rises and then falls.

Notice the pause between the in-breath and the out-breath.

Gently allow the gap between the breaths to increase by one or two seconds.

Continue to breathe normally in a relaxed manner. If any tension exists in the breathing, allow your breath to go back to a totally relaxed and comfortable breathing rate.

At the peak of your in-breath pause for three seconds, then breathe out.

At the end of your out-breath pause for three seconds, then breathe in.

Tips

- Keep your breathing relaxed at all times.
- When new to this practice, start in a quiet location to build up familiarity and confidence.

Common Problems

- "Distractions make me lose my concentration."

  Gentleness and a nonjudging attitude are key to this. If distractions arise, just gently and with great tenderness and love bring your attention back to your breathing.
- "I find it difficult to maintain focus."

  The temptation is to expend intense effort on focusing. As effort involves tension in the body, simply relax and playfully notice your breathing. It is natural for your attention to wander in the beginning.

TECHNIQUE FOUR: CHI GUNG BREATH FOR CALM

Background

This technique is from the Chi Gung tradition, started in China around the time of the first patriarch of Zen, Bodhidharma. It is believed he created these exercises in the Shoalin monastery in China. Believing his followers lacked vital energy and internal strength, he created a range of physical exercises that focus on creating energy in the body and then moving this energy throughout the body. This technique is part of a vast spectrum of Chi Gung postures from a range of different traditions.

Benefits

- Dramatically increases the body's energy
- Takes less than a minute

Technique

- Relax the muscles in your lower and upper belly.
- Breathe in and gently allow your stomach muscles to become full and rounded.
- Breathe out.
- Breathe in and quickly force your breath out in a short, sharp push through your nostrils.
- Take a quick short sharp breath in ... in less than a second.
- The sound should be like an old-fashioned bellows working quickly.
- Continue this for ten seconds while holding the posture. You should be able to make between twenty-eight and thirty-four out-breaths in ten seconds.
- After ten seconds take a long deep breath into your lower belly.

- As you breathe out, move your attention up your spine to the top of your head. Repeat this slow breathing for five breaths.
- Repeat another cycle of short, sharp, shallow quick breaths for another ten seconds.
- Again, slowly move your attention up your spine to the top of your head and this time bring your attention slowly down the front of your body to rest at your navel.

Tips
- The more strenuous the short in- and out-breaths the better.
- You know you are doing the exercise correctly when you feel out of breath after the ten seconds of short in- and out-breaths.
- The exercise can also be done sitting down.

Common Problems
- "Why do I move my attention up my spine?"
  The principle is that where your attention goes, energy flows. This naturally and automatically moves energy from your belly to your upper body.

9

The Path of the Present

The techniques in this chapter are:
  • Body Awareness
• Total Awareness
• Eating with Awareness
• Walking with Awareness
• Showering with Awareness
• Commuting with Awareness
• Total Awareness at the Gym

TECHNIQUE FIVE: BODY AWARENESS

Background

This technique comes from the Buddhist tradition of mindfulness.

Benefits

• Easy to do
• Reduces stress
• Can de done anywhere, anytime
• Benefits can be achieved in less than a minute
• Quickly increases the amount of meditation done every day
• Slows the mind

How this works:

- Attention is shifted away from your stressful thoughts. Effectively, you become uninterested in the mind.
- Your mind gridlocks when it becomes overloaded by the sea of sensations in your body.

Technique

- Take a deep breath in.
- Notice the sensations inside your body. Begin by noticing individual sensations inside in your belly, shoulders, neck, in the small muscles around the eyes, the forehead.
- Become curious about what sensations are there. Look for parts of your body that are experiencing:

Warmth	Tension
Coolness	Energy
Tingling	Movement
Openness	Quiet

- Notice any colors, sounds, melodies, tastes, or fragrances that are there.
- Widen your attention to include two or more areas at once, such as the belly and the shoulders, the forehead and the chest.
- Now widen your attention and become aware of all the sensations at once, as if your body were a single cell.

More experienced meditators: simply move to the last step.

Tips

Start in a quiet place and go through the exercise slowly step by step. It seems arduous, but the depth of the meditation is how wide your attention can be, how many sensations you can notice at the same time. The purpose is to build your capability until you can move to the last step, i.e. expand awareness to include all the sensations in your body at once.

One powerful way to improve the meditation is to ask questions about what sensations you are experiencing.

For example, ask yourself: What is happening now in my belly? What is happening to my shoulders? Describe to yourself what is happening there. How do the muscles in my chest feel? What's happening in my neck, in the small muscles around my eyes, in the muscles on my forehead? Are there any sensations of heat, warmth, coolness, tingling, or tightness anywhere? Even check for areas in the body where no sensation exists. No sensation is a sensation: the sensation of nothing.

Common Problems

• "I get bored."

There is nothing inherently interesting in the sensations you notice. The key is to become curious, like a child, and playfully notice as many sensations as you can. The more you notice, the quieter your mind becomes. Boredom is a natural process when you take your attention away from your mind. The key is to simply continue with the practice.

• "Am I doing this right?"

There is no right or wrong. There is no judgment. Whatever you notice is perfect. If you are simply noticing, you are doing this correctly.

• "I still have thoughts."

As long as you are in a body, you will have thoughts. The key is to relax. Let go of thoughts. When they appear, simply return to noticing sensations inside your body.

TECHNIQUE SIX: TOTAL AWARENESS

Background

This technique comes from the Buddhist tradition of mindfulness.

Benefits

- Easy to do.
- Reduces stress.
- Can de done anywhere, anytime.
- Benefits can be achieved in less than a minute.
- Quickly increases the amount of meditation done every day.
- This meditation powerfully slows the mind—the mind cannot exist when asked to notice everything inside and outside at the same time.

Technique

For beginners there are three steps to this meditation.

1 Take a deep breath in and out; close your eyes.

- Allow your attention to notice individual sensations inside your body.
- Notice sensations in your belly, your shoulders, your neck, in the small muscles around the eyes, the anus, the forehead.
- Notice any tastes that are there.
- Widen your attention to include two or more areas at once, such as the belly and the shoulders, the forehead and the chest.
- Now widen your attention and become aware of all the sensations at once.

2 Take a deep breath in and out.

- Allow your attention to notice individual experiences outside your body.
- What can you see? Name them to yourself.
- What can you hear? Note what sounds are present.
- What can you smell? Note what fragrances are there.
- What tastes are there?
- What sensations are there? Notice what your body is in contact with.
- Allow your eyes to become unfocused and take all of this in at once.

3 Cast your awareness wide to take in everything at the same time.
- Inside you
- Outside you

More experienced meditators, simply move to step three.

You may initially want to look at individual points inside and outside, such as the color of a rose and the inside sensation of your belly, or the different pairs of inside/outside sensations—such as the fragrance and your shoulders, the colors outside and the muscles in your forehead. Eventually, become aware of all experiences outside and inside you at the same time.

Tips

Start in a quiet place and go through the exercise slowly step by step. It seems arduous, but the depth of the meditation is how wide your attention can be, how many inside/outside sensations you notice at the same time.

The purpose is to build your capability until you can move to the last step, i.e. expand awareness, to include inside/outside sensations at the same time.

One powerful way to improve the meditation is to ask questions about what sensations you are experiencing.

Inside: For example, ask yourself, what is happening now in my belly? What is happening to my shoulders? Describe to yourself what is happening there. How do the muscles in my chest feel? What's happening in my neck, in the small muscles around my eyes, in the muscles on my forehead? Are there any sensations of heat, warmth, coolness, tingling, or tightness anywhere? Even check for areas in the body where no sensation exists. No sensation is a sensation … the sensation of nothing.

Outside: Ask yourself, what items can you see? Breathe from your lower belly and as you breathe in and out, gracefully and gently notice the color, scents, sounds, and sensations. Allow your eyes to become unfocused and take all of this in at once.

Common Problems
- "I get bored."

    This is a natural process when we take our attention away from our mind. The key is to simply continue with the practice.
- "Am I doing this right?"

    If you are simply noticing, you are doing this correctly.
- "I still have thoughts."

    As long as you are in a body, you will have thoughts. The key is to relax. Let go of thoughts. When they appear, simply return to noticing sensations inside and outside you at the same time.

●

On thoughts:

"Pay no attention. Don't fight them. Just do nothing about them,
let them be, whatever they are. Your very fighting them
gives them strength. Just disregard. Look through."

SRI NISARGADATTA MAHARAJ

"What is Buddha?A Buddha is one who lies 24 hours in mindfulness."

THICH NHAT HANH

●

TECHNIQUE SEVEN: EATING WITH AWARENESS

Background
This technique stems from the Buddhist tradition of mindfulness.

Benefits
- Easy to do
- Can de done at any mealtime
- Benefits can be achieved in less than a minute
- Quickly increases the amount of meditation done every day
- Slows the mind

How this works:
- Attention is shifted away from your stressful thoughts.
- Your mind gridlocks when it becomes overloaded by the sea of sensations inside and outside of you.

Technique
As you sit down to eat, notice the sensations inside your body.

1 Check in with your body. How is it feeling? What sensations are there? Scan your body by noticing individual sensations inside in your belly, shoulders, neck, in the small muscles around the eyes, the forehead. Look for sensations of:

Warmth	Tension
Coolness	Energy
Tingling	Movement
Openness	Quiet

2 Now widen your attention and become aware of all the sensations at once, as if your body were a single cell.

3 Now notice sensations outside your body.

4 Notice the food before you. Notice the colors, textures, tastes, and fragrances that are there.

5 Now notice the food before you and notice the sensations in your body at the same time.

More experienced meditators, simply move to the last step.

Tips

• Eat slowly. Lift the food slowly to your mouth as you keep noticing all the sensations.

• Take a few moments to chew slowly.

• Pause before each mouthful to really notice the taste of the food.

Common Problems

• "I'm always in such a hurry. Mealtime for me is usually done in five minutes!"

Whenever you eat, simply play with as many of the practice tips as you can. Start small—take only a few pauses before mouth-fuls. Take only a few mouthfuls in slow motion. Then increase these each day until you find the right balance between "eating with awareness" and eating in a hurry.

- "But what I notice is so boring—it's just simple sensations. Who cares if I notice the color of the food? This can't be meditation!"

Remember: meditation is a journey beyond your mind. Your core, essence, and heart are experienced when you go beyond the mind. This technique powerfully allows your mind to slow by flooding it with sensations.

Boredom is your mind screaming for attention. In meditation, boredom is a sign that your meditation is working. It's a sign that you're learning to shift your attention away from your mind, which wants complex puzzles to solve. With this technique you transform each meal into an oasis of calm and take a much need-ed break from your frenetically racing mind.

- "I still have thoughts."

As long as you are in a body, you will have thoughts. The key is to relax. Let go of thoughts. When they appear, simply return to noticing sensations.

TECHNIQUE EIGHT: WALKING WITH AWARENESS
Background
This technique stems from the Buddhist tradition of mindfulness.

Benefits
- Easy to do
- Reduces stress

- Can de done anywhere, anytime
- Benefits can be achieved in less than a minute
- Transforms the street into an ocean of calm

Technique
This technique builds on the Total Awareness technique and provides instructions on how to do this while walking.

1 Notice what is outside your body.
- What can you see? Name what you see to yourself.
- What can you hear? Note what sounds are present.
- What can you smell? Note what fragrances are there.
- What tastes are there?
- What sensations are there?

2 Allow your eyes to become unfocused and take all of this in at once.

3 Notice experiences inside your body.
- Notice the feeling of your feet on the pavement.
- Notice the pace of your breathing.
- Notice the sensations in your belly, shoulders, neck, the small muscles around the eyes, the forehead.
- Now widen your attention and become aware of all the sensations at once.

4 Cast your awareness wide to take in everything at the same time.
- Inside you
- Outside you

More experienced meditators, simply move to the last step.

Tips
- Always be safe and aware of the outside environment.
- Start in relatively quiet streets where it's easy and safe to notice sensations.

Common Problems
- "I get distracted easily."

   Don't be discouraged. Start slowly and gently and gradually increase the amount of time you focus.
- "Sometimes I feel spacey and unfocused when I do this."

   This can occur in the beginning. Eventually you will get used to being able to move safely and easily while doing this practice.

TECHNIQUE NINE: SHOWERING WITH AWARENESS
Background
This technique stems from the Buddhist tradition of mindfulness.

Benefits
- Simple to do.
- Reduces stress.
- Benefits can be achieved in less than a minute.
- Stops the mind—the mind cannot cope when asked to notice everything inside and outside at the same time.

Technique
In the morning shower:

1 Allow your attention to notice individual experiences outside your body.

• What can you see?

• What can you hear? Listen to the sound of the water.

• What can you smell? Notice the fragrance of soaps and shampoos.

• What sensations are there? Notice the luxurious sensations as you clean and pamper your body.

2 Notice experiences inside your body.

• How do your belly, shoulders, neck, buttocks, legs, and arms feel as you bathe them?

• Now widen your attention and become aware of all the sensations at once.

3 Cast your awareness wide to take in everything at the same time.

• Inside you

• Outside you

More experienced meditators, simply move to step three.

Tips

• Make a conscious decision—this is a time for you to ignore thoughts and take a complete break from your mind. If thousands of thoughts about your day rush in, then simply choose to return to them later, and focus on the practice.

• Use Tai Chi showering—move your body in slow motion and really notice the sensations that are there.

• Take a few moments to be still, close your eyes, and notice how

THE PATH OF THE PRESENT

all of your body responds.

- Sing! Notice the vibration in your throat, chest, mouth, and other parts of your body.

Common Problems

"I use the shower as a time to think about my day."

No problem—use this technique when it's useful, such as when you want to take a break from your mind. Often surprising and creative solutions to your problems arrive when your mind is more relaxed.

TECHNIQUE TEN: COMMUTING WITH AWARENESS

Background

This technique stems from the Buddhist tradition of mindfulness.

Benefits

- Easy to do.
- Reduces stress.
- Benefits can be achieved in less than a minute.
- Transform your commute from a time of worry into an opportunity to be effortless, limitless, and infinite.

Technique

This uses the Total Awareness technique with specific instructions for commuting.

1 On your morning commute take a deep breath in and out. When you can, close your eyes.

- Notice sensations inside your body.
- Notice sensations in your belly, your shoulders, your neck, in the

small muscles around the eyes, the anus, the forehead.

- Widen your attention to include two or more areas at once, such as the belly and the shoulders, the forehead and the chest.
- Now widen your attention and become aware of all the sensations at once.

2 Take a deep breath, then allow your eyes to open.

- What can you see? Name what you can see to yourself.
- What can you hear? Note what sounds, melodies, and harmonies are present on your commute.
- What can you smell? Note what fragrances are there.
- What tastes are there?
- What sensations are there? Notice contact of your body with the chair.
- Allow your eyes to become unfocused and take all of this in at once.

3 Cast your awareness wide to take in everything at the same time.

- Inside you
- Outside you

More experienced meditators, simply move to step three.

Tips

- Always be safe and aware of the outside environment.
- Start small, by spending a few minutes a day practicing the technique.
- In the end, your commute can be a chance to feel infinite, endless, boundless, and vast.

Common Problems

"I normally use my commute to read/prepare for the day/update my to-do list/sleep."

No problem—do what is most useful. Scientific research has shown that the above technique is a powerful way to reduce chronic pain, stress, and anxiety attacks. Play with the technique and see if there is more or less benefit using part of your commute for meditation.

●

"Some people get on the bus and just sit on the bus.
I get on the bus and practice my yoga (meditation practice)."

DANIEL ODIER

●

TECHNIQUE ELEVEN: TOTAL AWARENESS AT THE GYM

Background

Total Awareness at the Gym is based on the Buddhist tradition of mindfulness.

Benefits

• Can be used to clear and express strong emotions from the day
• Safe way to experience and express intense emotions
• Powerfully slows the mind and reduces stress
• Uses all of the body
• Can be used when doing any exercise

Technique

To slow the mind: The gym is a great place to easily be aware of the sensations in the body—noticing everything inside your body and outside your body at the same time, while continuing to breathe deeply.

To express: Feel the sensations in your body and allow yourself to experience whatever emotions are there. As you feel these emotions, bring their energy into your aerobic exercises. For example, if feeling anger, allow the emotion to be expressed by running, cycling, or swimming as a way of feeling and expressing this anger.

At the end of your session in the changing room, sit down, close your eyes, and allow your mind to be calm.

Tips

Be safe! Ensure you can safely focus on your exercise. Sometimes the awareness meditation can leave people feeling "spacey" and unfocused. Your physical safety is paramount; ensure you can safely focus on your physical exercise.

Don't use your workout to try and not feel your stressful emotions. Use the exercise to get into your feelings and let them be expressed.

Common Problems

"Sometimes I feel I'm 'not in my body' when I use awareness to capture everything inside and outside at the same time."

This sometimes happens when first using the Total Awareness meditation. The most important aspect at the gym is your physical safety. If feeling dizzy or spaced out, then stop the practice to ensure you can focus just on your exercise. After some practice, the meditation becomes second nature; you know when you need to bring attention back to the exercise and when it can be cast wide to include everything inside and outside at the same time.

10

The Path of Remembering

Similar to prayer beads, rosary beads, or malas—which remind you to recite prayers—the following techniques are like anchors calling you to calm, bliss, love, and compassion.

TECHNIQUE TWELVE: ANCHORS I

Background

There are three main inspirations for this technique.

- Neuro Linguistic Programming—for its powerful work on anchors.
- Hindu hand positions (called *mudras*)—Hindus use these to recognize different meanings. Many Buddhist and Hindu statues have gods with specific hand positions.
- Chinese acupuncture indicates that connecting the thumb and forefinger connects meridians that are helpful.

Benefits

- Creates emotional states in an instant.
- Can create feelings such as calm, strength, an ability to handle anything, and confidence.
- Once built, you can use the anchor anytime, anywhere.

Technique

There are two stages to this technique.

1 Building the anchor:

Sit in a relaxed position at home.

Think of the emotional state you wish to create (such as any of those listed previously).

Close your eyes and remember a time when you felt the desired feeling most intensely. As you remember the feeling, keep building up the emotion by replaying the memory. Step back into the memory and move your body as if you were re-living the experience.

For example, to create confidence, remember a time when you were totally confident.

How would you breathe if you were completely confident?

What tone of voice would you use if you were totally confident?

How would you be sitting if your whole body was filled with confidence?

What thoughts would you be thinking as an awesomely confident person?

When the feeling of confidence is at its most intense, place your thumb and forefinger together.

Repeat these steps as frequently as possible.

2 Using the anchor:

Whenever you need, place the thumb and forefinger together, and the feeling of confidence, in the above example, will come back. If the anchor is not effective, rebuild it.

Tips

There are two criteria for success in building the anchor.

1 The intensity of the emotional state:

- Build the emotional state by memory and body posture.
- Use music that inspires you.
- Talk to yourself as an encouraging coach.
- Remember images from films when you felt the same feeling.
- Remember powerful feelings from books you've read.
- Dare to imagine. Ask yourself, "If anything were possible, if there were no barriers at all, how would I be?"

   Use all of the above to build the emotional state to its highest.

2 Placing the thumb and forefinger together at the *peak* of the experience:

   When you feel the desired emotion most powerfully, *then* use the anchor. If you anchor too early, or too late, the anchor is less effective.

Common Problems

- "Won't people notice me when I use the anchor in public?"
   I've used this anchor thousands of times, particularly for being calm yet powerful in stressful situations, and no one has noticed.
- "It kind of works but I don't feel the emotion strongly enough."
   Rebuild the anchor at home.

TECHNIQUE THIRTEEN: ANCHORS II
Benefits

Uses everyday items to create anchors

Technique

PC Screensaver: Create a screensaver that suggests calmness, a mantra, a reminder to breathe, a reminder to become aware.

Cell Phone: Use the welcome note as a mantra, a blessing, a call to be aware, a command to love all.

Personal Digital Assistant: Place a post-it note inside with a suggestion to bless all around you, to "Be Aware Now." Set the alarm to beep every half hour to remind you to do the awareness meditation.

Tips

• Make the anchors/reminders short and simple.
• Make them things that will remind you to practice.

11

The Path of Heart

This path focuses on meditations that build heart energy and reconnect you to life.

TECHNIQUE FOURTEEN: MAGNIFY HEART ENERGY

Background

Focus techniques are a major part of Hindu and Buddhist spiritual traditions. Masters can keep their attention on a single point until they become "one pointed," which means totally absorbed in the object upon which they are meditating, effortlessly and without distraction.

Many Eastern spiritual traditions refer to different energy centers, called *chakras*. There are seven different centers, each with different qualities, frequencies, and vibrations. Each chakra is associated with certain deities, mantras, and mudras.

Benefits

- Magnifies qualities of:

Wisdom	Love
Inspiration	Creativity
Intuition	Compassion and Calm

- Powerful doorway to your heart
- Can be done anywhere, anytime

Technique

Practice this exercise at home.

Sit and place your hands together in a "prayer" position in front of your chest.

Spend a few minutes noticing what sensations, experiences, sounds, colors, fragrances, and textures are there.

Keep your attention on the center of your chest.

This point is a doorway into a center of energy called a chakra, which in turn is a doorway into your heart.

How this works:

One of the Laws of Meditation is "What you notice, you magnify. What you worship, you become."

By simply placing your attention on your heart center, you magnify the quality of energy that is there—automatically, effortlessly, and naturally. Whether you know it or not, whether you feel it or not, your heart energy starts to build.

Tips

- When you first try this at home, play relaxing music and light candles.
- The benefits are a function of time—so maximize the time by placing your attention on your heart as you walk, commute, shower, eat, sing, talk, and relax.
- Keep your attention on your heart for as much of the day as you like. Your heart area becomes the "default" resting place for your

attention, rather than your mind. Even short amounts of placing your attention on your heart center have benefits.

- Keep your hands in the "prayer" position or touch your physical heart as a reminder—this helps magnify the energy.

12

The Path of Focus

This meditation uses focus to build wisdom, clarity, and calm.

TECHNIQUE FIFTEEN: MAGNIFY WISDOM

Background

Focus techniques are a major part of Hindu and Buddhist spiritual traditions. This technique is derived from the same tradition as the previous technique.

Benefits

- Magnifies qualities of wisdom, clarity, calmness, insight, intuition
- Powerful doorway to your essence
- Can be done anywhere, anytime

Technique

Practice this exercise at home.

Sit and place a finger onto the space in the center of your eyebrows.

Spend a few minutes noticing what sensations, experiences, sounds, colors, fragrances, and textures are there.

Keep your attention on your third eye.

117

This point is a doorway into a center of energy called a chakra, which in turn is a doorway into your core.

How this works:
One of the Laws of Meditation is "What you notice, you magnify. What you worship, you become."

By simply placing your attention on your third eye, you magnify the quality of energy that is there—automatically, effortlessly, and naturally. Whether you know it or not, whether you feel it or not, the energy of your third eye starts to build.

Tips
- When you first try this at home, play relaxing music and light candles.
- The benefits are a function of time—so increase the amount of time by placing your attention on your third eye whenever you are seated.
- Even short amounts of time placing your attention on your third eye have benefits.
- Occasionally touch your third eye as a reminder—this helps magnify the energy.

13

The Path of Open Body

The techniques in this chapter are:
 • The Open Body
• Chi Gung for Stress Release
• Bonus Technique: Dealing with Anger

The following techniques powerfully transform Effort into Effortlessness.

TECHNIQUE SIXTEEN: THE OPEN BODY

Background

This technique stems from the Tantra tradition. Tantra tradition emphasizes that a relaxed, open, and fluid body is able to carry more energy. The belief is that kinks, blockages, and contractions limit our ability to feel our essence, core, and heart. From a Western standpoint, this is a form of progressive muscle relaxation.

Benefits

• Quickly creates calm
• Releases tension stored in the body

- Makes the journey to your core effortless
- Proven to create benefits in less than a minute

Technique

This technique changes our response to stressful situations. By deliberately relaxing your muscles, you effectively break the pattern of stress that requires our bodies to close and contract.

- Notice the muscles in your shoulders. See if there is any tension there. You may want to hunch your shoulders toward your ears and then relax them to get an idea of the level of stress.
- Notice the small muscles around your eyes. Allow them to relax. You may need to squint, blink, and even gently massage this area to really allow them to relax.
- Now allow the muscles in your forehead to relax. Again you may want to put the book down and gently massage your forehead and your temples.
- Now notice the muscles in your neck. If it is safe for you to do, gently allow your head to roll from side to side.
- Notice your jaw muscles. Deliberately soften the jaw and allow it to loosen and remain gently open.
- Now notice the muscles in your belly. To do this, take one deep and full breath from your belly. Take another deep breath, this time while keeping your chest and shoulders still—this allows more air into your belly. Take one more deep breath and use your abdominal muscles to actually push the belly out. Then relax and notice whether there is a greater sense of ease and relaxation in your stomach muscles.

When you become familiar with this technique, it can take less than thirty seconds to do.

Tips

- Spend one minute a day choosing to relax your body. Increase the amount over time. Eventually this is an ongoing practice that can be done throughout the day.
- Pick three areas that hold the most tension for you. For example, your jaw, belly, and the small muscles around the eye. Focus on relaxing these three areas.

Common Problems

"I've been doing this for some time and my body *still* holds tension."

It takes dedicated daily practice for the body to become used to operating in a relaxed and open manner. We have a lifetime habit of tightening and closing our bodies.

●

"Only when the front of your body is relaxed and opened,
your breath full and deep …
can your fullest intelligence
manifest spontaneously in the situation."

DAVID DEIDA

●

TECHNIQUE SEVENTEEN: CHI GUNG FOR CALM

Background

This technique uses Chi Gung movements. Chi Gung is an ancient Taoist practice that means "cultivation of the *chi*," or energy.

Benefits
- Quickly creates calm
- Powerfully releases the tension of your day
- Significant benefits in less than a minute

Technique

Stand with your feet shoulder-width apart.

Bend your knees slightly.

Put your hands by your side with palms facing forward.

Take a long deep breath in.

In time with your in-breath, clench your fists and bring them toward your chin, with your elbows almost touching. The stance is similar to a boxer's.

Hold your breath for three seconds.

Exhale, unclench your fists, relax your fingers and chest, and bring your hands by your side with palms facing outward.

Do this five times.

Tips
- Feel the stress and tension of your day. Express this tension by tightening the muscles in all of your body, particularly the face, chest, arms, and shoulders.
- As you exhale, release the tensions of the day and allow your body to relax open.

BONUS TECHNIQUE: DEALING WITH ANGER

Background

Sometimes I have been very angry and stressed at work. Safely expressing anger releases steam from the system. The only other options appear to be:

- Keeping in the anger and stewing over it for ages (watch what this does to your body!)
- Taking this out on others

Unsurprisingly, neither of these options are helpful.

I learned this meditation from the Sahaja Yoga School, led by Shri Mataji Nirmala Devi.

Benefits

- Allows anger to be experienced fully and not suppressed
- Provides a safe channel for anger to be expressed

Technique

- Find a quiet place at home where you will not be disturbed.
- Spend one minute noticing all the sensations outside your body (what you see, taste, touch, hear, and smell).
- Spend one minute noticing all the sensations inside your body (what you see, taste, touch, hear, and smell).
- Become aware of the sensation of anger within your body. This is a meditation based on the body. We cannot feel anger without our bodies reacting in specific ways.
- Thoughts about the situation with which, or person with whom, you are angry will arise. The key is to notice not the situation/person/issues causing the anger but the sensations anger has created within your body. This is not a time for the mind to work on the anger, analyze situations, or create solutions. Take a pillow, a shoe,

123

or twist a bathroom towel into the shape of a rope. Feel into the anger and beat the floor with the pillow/shoe/towel. Make the statement, "I am angry ... " and let the anger out through your body and into the floor. If appropriate, use your voice out loud to express anger. Allow whatever anger is there to be expressed through your body.

- Continue this until you no longer need to.
- Become grounded again by noticing the sensations outside your body and inside your body at the same time. Ask the question, "What can I do to constructively use this energy?" Sit quietly and see if any response comes.

Important: Do not imagine other people while doing this practice. This includes neither visualizing them nor using their names. The purpose is not to do energetic violence, harm, or send negative energy to others. The practice is looking into your own body and expressing, "I am angry." It is not outward-looking at others.

Tips

- Do the meditation as often and for as long as you need to.
- A different version of this technique is excellent to use while running, swimming, or cycling: getting in touch with sensations of anger in the body and allowing the body to express this energy in vigorous movement.

Common Problems

- "It's difficult for me to find a quiet place to do this."

    Often the bedroom is the best place. Sometimes you have to be practical and ask others not to disturb you for half an hour and put on loud music to muffle the sounds!

• "Sometimes I am so angry with a specific person, it's hard not to imagine shouting angry things to them directly."

It is natural for us to identify the cause or supposed source of our anger—a person, a situation, a group of people. The key to this meditation is to move from the cause to how this is experienced in the body. As humans we are linked energetically—what we think inside affects the outside. Whenever the meditation moves away from our bodily sensations and becomes about another person or group of people, we run the risk of energetically expressing anger/violence to them.

To help you notice anger in your body, there are two sets of questions.

Firstly ask yourself, "Where am I feeling this anger? What is happening in my belly when I think of this person, situation, or group of people? How do my neck and shoulder muscles react?"

Secondly, ask yourself, "How does my body want to move when I experience this anger? What do my hands and arms want to do when I connect with this anger?"

What is important is to drive the attention back to the bodily sensations.

●

"Formula for Life:
Become Grounded,
Experience,
Express."
KEN MELLOR

●

14

The Path of Visualization

The techniques in this chapter are:
- White Light
- Seeing the Good in All People

TECHNIQUE EIGHTEEN: WHITE LIGHT

Background

The White Light meditation is from the Buddhist tradition.

Benefits
- Reduces stress
- Promotes a sense of calm and well-being
- Increases a sense of connectedness with others

Technique

Sit in a quiet location and breathe from your belly.

Imagine a white light in the center of your heart. The light represents healing, calm, purity, and universal love.

Gradually imagine the light becoming more radiant, more brilliant, and more vibrant. Feel blessed by the light.

Gently imagine the light gradually expanding to fill your whole heart, then your body.

Now imagine your body is filled to overflowing with white light, so much so that the light radiates from you and into the room.

Imagine the room being filled with light that then pours out into the world.

Spend ten minutes doing this.

Common Problems

- "I have difficulty creating images in my mind."

    Some people respond more to feelings or sounds.

    If healing, calm, and love were a feeling, where in your body would you feel this sensation the most? Magnify the feeling. Make it deepen, expand, and fill all of your system.

    If sounds make more sense—what sound or melody do you associate with healing, calm, and love? Allow the sound to become louder, more intense, sweeter, and richer until it resonates through every cell in your body.

- "It's difficult to concentrate on breathing *and* use the imagination."

    Concentration often means effort, and the key to all meditations is to relax. If you are contracting or becoming tense, just gently allow yourself to relax. Use the belly breath at the start of the meditation, then use your imagination.

Tips

- Imagine you are watching a film with the image of your body on the screen, and your heart is slowly filling with light. Step into the image on the screen and feel the light filling your heart.

TECHNIQUE NINETEEN: SEEING THE GOOD IN ALL PEOPLE

Background

Leaning to see the good in others is a key teaching in many traditions.

Benefits

- Improves relationships with difficult people.
- Can be used at work and during busy situations.
- Increases the feeling of connectedness with all people.
- Once the structure has been mastered, the benefits can be achieved in less than a minute.

Technique

There are two stages to this meditation. First build the framework at home and then use it at the office or wherever you need it.

At home:

- Sit in a quiet place.
- Bring to mind a quality (such as peace, calm, love, oneness …) or a deity. Alternatively you can simply imagine a white light. If using a quality, simply see the word written or create a symbol.
- Feel in your body what it means to be filled with such a quality or with the deity. Imagine your whole body filled with this deity, this quality, or this beautiful white light.
- Now ground yourself by noticing all sensations inside and outside you at the same time.
- Bring to mind a picture of the person with whom you desire a closer relationship.
- Imagine the deity or quality in the middle of the person's heart.

Imagine the quality/deity as a symbol or simply as a word written on the person's heart. Imagine a white light appearing in the middle of the person's heart.

- Now allow the image of the deity, or the symbol or quality or the light to start to increase in size until it fills the whole person's body.
- Affirm, "I love, honor, and recognize your true nature." Other affirmations are:

> "I acknowledge the Divine within you."
> "I affirm your true depth and goodness."
> "I relate to the god within you."

At work:

When meeting the person, imagine the deity, quality, light within the person's heart. Some people may need to close their eyes briefly; others can softly allow their eyes to become unfocused and imagine this picture within.

- Quickly say one of the affirmations internally.
- When you meet the person communicate as if you were communicating to the person's highest truth, deepest nature, to the god within them, to the source of all beings.

Beginner

- At home create the image of the Divine within the person with whom you wish a better relationship.
- Say the affirmation, "I love, honor, and recognize your true nature."

Intermediate

- Before meeting the person, have the intention to communicate with the core of the other person.

- Briefly close your eyes and recall the picture of the deity centered in the heart of the person.
- Say the affirmation, "I love, honor, and recognize your true nature."

Advanced

- Before you begin to communicate with the other person, notice your breathing and again have the intention to communicate to the core of the other person.
- While listening, you can again repeat the affirmation.
- You can again briefly create/imagine the deity within the other person.

Tips

- Imagining a picture and saying the affirmation can take the briefest moment. The importance is having the intention of communicating directly with the person's deepest core.
- Keep breathing from the belly before you connect with this person.

Common Problems

- "Do I need to have a clear image when I meet this person?"

  Clear images come with practice. The key is the intention to communicate to the deepest level of the person, a level beyond the surface personality.

- "How do I 'communicate to the deity within?'"

  Set an anchor such as a hand mudra. Say the name of the quality/deity before you speak. Put your attention briefly on the person's physical heart. Talk normally, but your attention is briefly put on:

The person's physical heart
Saying the deity's name
Visualizing the deity
Repeating the deity's name

P.S. Our attention and our capacity to remember pictures is lightning fast; the above four steps can take as few as three to four seconds over a whole conversation.

15

The Ideal Day: Putting It All Together

Here's an example of how you could create an oasis of calm and bliss in your day:

6:00 AM: You awake. You build vitality and energy in your body with a set of Chi Gung breaths for energy.

6:10 AM: Feeling more alive, you write down a list of action points for the day, as a way to manage them.

6:15 AM: You shower and access the ocean of calm through a Total Awareness practice. Thoughts of your day appear in your mind. You notice them and return to the practice. You start to see the tendency of your mind to race and panic about the day.

6:30 AM: You add some more points to this to-do list.

6:35 AM: You eat a quick breakfast at home. To break the pattern of over-thinking and focusing on stressful thoughts, you quiet and enliven your mind with a grounding technique. After many years of practice you'll begin to see how your entire day was spent chasing thoughts. You'll be grateful that you now have the tools to create an oasis of calm whenever you want.

7:00 AM: You walk to the station. You start to plan your day, using the time to mentally run through important items. You reduce the tension of the day through a few power breaths. You create a feeling of power, confidence, calm, poise, and energy through using an anchoring technique. You turn on your cell phone and see another reminder to be calm. You take a few breaths and combine this with a Body Awareness technique to create mental clarity.

7:10 AM: On the subway you notice all the situations that used to create stress: the crowds, the pushing, the heat, and the noise. You smile and access an oasis of calm using the Total Awareness technique. You close your eyes and spend five minutes magnifying the feeling of love and connectedness by focusing on your heart. Using the Path of Visualization, you imagine white healing light blessing the passengers on the train. Thoughts often interrupt the practice and you smile gently to yourself and return to the practice. You have given up the idea of success or failure in meditation and see every distraction as a way to relax, breathe, and return to the practice. It's unlike anything you've ever tried in your life. You spend five minutes sending white light to your loved ones.

You turn on your BlackBerry and see another anchor to create calm. The rest of the trip you spend thinking about work, reading through some memos.

7:30 AM: You arrive at work fresh, calm, focused, and alert. You turn on your computer and see a screensaver that reminds you to breathe deeply from your belly.

7:35 AM: You attend a meeting with your boss—two quick power breaths to remain grounded and to lower heart and respiratory rate.

8:00 AM: You have a meeting with a person you find challenging.

• You create a sense of calm, ease, and focus with two power breaths.

- You place your attention on your heart as a way to build heart energy.
- You use an anchor (thumb and forefinger together) to create confidence, power, and drive.
- You focus 100 percent on the meeting at hand.
- The meeting goes like a breeze; the difficult person senses an ease within.

The next three hours are spent totally focused on delivering on your work objectives.

11:30 AM: A stressful situation arises:
- You use Body Awareness and Total Awareness to feel all of the situation.
- You take a power breath.
- You reduce the level of stress by relaxing your body open rather than contracting it.
- You remain calm.
- As you are more relaxed, your memory is better, your mind is clear, and it's easy to see the way forward.
  You take a two-minute break to clear your mind and send your attention wide as a way to "feel" beyond the confines of your body.
  In the bathroom you do a quiet Chi Gung breath, relaxing key stress points in his body.
  You have mastered the Total Awareness technique, which enables you to feel toward the edges of the horizon and beyond. This instantly creates a sense of deep peace and calm as your mind takes a much-needed break.

12:30 PM: Lunch. You take a brief moment to do the Total Awareness meditation to relax your mind and create greater clarity and focus.

12:45 PM: As you walk back to work, you stop to connect to your heart. You do this by simply placing your attention there. During this time thoughts continually appear—you have mastered your mind; you allow them to be there and choose which ones will help you with your job, which ones are to be ignored. Your primary focus is on your heart. You feel your heart energy increase, and a sense of love and calm arises. You pass a stranger and your heart says smile, so you do—even though it doesn't make logical sense to do it. The stranger smiles back—and intuitively feels an aliveness of energy in you, although that stranger doesn't know why.

Other people can feel your calm and energy.

You feel wide and disappear for a moment, lost in the moment, and the core of your being starts to flow through you. Irrationally, feelings of bliss, love, compassion, and oneness start to flow. You then decide that irrational joy and bliss is what you want. This takes ten minutes.

1:00 PM: Your cell phone rings. You see the message "Breathe" and realize in your bliss you have held your breath. You smile at the omission, not berating yourself for having forgotten and continue to do your power breaths.

You check your PDA, which has "Be Calm Now ... " written on the top. You smile and continue to do the breath practice.

1:00–5:00 PM: The next four hours are back-to-back meetings in which superior performance requires 100 percent focus on your job. You easily drop all practice to totally deliver superior performance.

Afterwards you write up some minutes; part of your attention is on your core, part is on your job. You flicker attention between 100 percent focus on your task and on the ocean of calm. Then artfully and with total appropriateness you discern when work requires 100 percent focus.

Even walking between meetings you can feel wide to the edges of the building, your body, and then back. This takes a few seconds, but delivers a calmer mind. During momentary breaks you spend part of your attention on your heart, in a flickering fashion. You know that attention is instantaneous—so even an instant kiss of your heart with your attention can enliven it.

Your attention can now be split—you keep some attention on your core, and some on your work. Your attention is primarily on your job, knowing this is not a separation from your core, but part of it.

5:30 PM: Your intuition suggests a course of action. You have perfected your intuition over a number of years. You prudently check your decision out with a few others. It turns out to be the correct course of action. You silently give thanks to your heart for providing the answer.

7:00 PM: The commute home is a time to practice Total Awareness and write up some notes on work.

7:30 PM: You return home with most of the stress of the day gone. You greet your loved ones with greater presence, awareness, and love.

The above may sound like too many activities. It's a bit like driving a car; there are many different tasks—check rearview mirror, brakes, speed indicator, gears, etc. But after a while it becomes automatic, natural, and effortless.

open-eyed zen

"You can't do it in a minute!" she said, smiling.

It was my sister talking to me. I'd just told her about the title of my book. I love my sister—so full of energy and vibrancy. She also has very little interest in spiritual things. She is incredibly practical.

"Really? Are you sure?" she continued, enjoying the fact that her practicality was right. And enjoying how her big brother may have made a disastrous mistake in leaving banking to write a meditation book on something that, she thought, might not work.

"But meditation means sitting in lotus positions! They have their eyes closed. This can't be true. On the subway, on the street? That can't be true—it's totally noisy, crowded. It's the last place anyone would meditate!"

I agreed. "I understand how you think like that. I thought the same way for many years. Even after fifteen years of meditation, I thought all meditations were sitting down. That was until I learned about the Eye of Zen."

"The Eye of Zen? What's that?"

"Do you remember the time I was struggling as a banker"? I reminded her of when I was twenty-four years old, had just been made a manager, and clearly wasn't up to the new responsibility. My stress levels soared. I started to lose my hair. I was grinding my teeth so hard at night my dentist told me to wear a mouth guard. I was going to be bald and toothless by thirty!

She smiled. Family always seems to smile at the messy side of life.

"I wondered about what stress was doing on the inside. I became concerned. Something had to be done. So I spent many years researching Zen traditions. I noticed that Zen monks spend about 40 percent of their day in seated meditations. I wondered: What do they do for the rest of the day? They don't sit down for the whole day, so what do they do? Can they meditate while working in the garden or doing their chores? That's when I learned about Open-Eyed Zen."

It's a Zen technique that has been spoken about for many centuries, and has recently been made popular in the West by Gurdjieff, Barry Long, Ram Dass, Eckhart Tolle, and Ken Mellor.

"It was a relief to discover that Zen can be practiced with the eyes open and while moving. It could easily be called Moving Zen."

My sister was still incredulous.

"It's a technique to allow the mind to stop and become still—even while moving about in the world. My teacher showed me that there were a number of gems inside my body I could collect. And there were treasures on the outside I could experience, if only I knew where to look."

My sister became interested in the story. She put down the BBQ steak and the glass of white wine and began to listen.

"What are the treasures? Where do we find the gems?"

I started to laugh. "They aren't physical gems, but they are more valuable than diamonds. Here, let me show you."

Inner Gems	Outer Treasures
Sight	Sight
Sound	Sound
Smell	Smell
Sensations	Touch
Taste	Taste
Total Riches = The Present	

The more inner gems and outer treasures you collect, the more the mind becomes still. It works because the mind becomes so flooded with sensations on the inside and outside that it gridlocks and stops. The mind starts again the moment you stop the practice. You become plugged into the present moment.

If this technique doesn't work then you need to gather more inner gems and more outer treasures. Your mind cannot work when saturated with sensations.

ABOUT THE AUTHOR

Mark Thornton has combined twenty-two years of spiritual seeking with fourteen years work in investment banking. His last post was as a Vice President and Chief Operating Officer for an American investment bank in London.

Born to Australian parents in 1965, he was raised in Melbourne, attended a Jesuit school, and has a degree in Economics. He lives in New York and teaches international corporations Eastern relaxation techniques.

He is the Project Director for The Global Health Institute, a non-profit organization that aims to unlock the human value of capital. He directs a project to teach and test the bottom line impact to companies on implementing Eastern techniques to create drive, focus, and productivity.

To learn more about Mark Thornton and his work, please go to www.yescalm.org.

SOUNDS TRUE was founded in 1985 with a clear vision: to disseminate spiritual wisdom. Located in Boulder, Colorado, Sounds True publishes teaching programs that are designed to educate, uplift, and inspire. With more than 600 titles available, we work with many of the leading spiritual teachers, thinkers, healers, and visionary artists of our time.

For a free catalog, or for more information on audio programs by Mark Thornton, please contact Sounds True at www.soundstrue.com, call us toll-free at 800-333-9185, or write

The Sounds True Catalog
PO Box 8010
Boulder CO 80306

MEDITATION INTENSIVE TRAINING
Certificate

Mark Thornton and Project Bliss invite you
and one companion to attend the Meditation
Mastery Seminar, as complimentary guests.
To register and for more information go to
www.yescalm.org

If you have no access to a computer, call toll-free:
888 YES CALM (1 888 937 2256)

The offer is open to all purchasers of *Meditation in a New York Minute* by Mark Thornton. Original proof of purchase is required (receipt number, paypal confirmation, Amazon.com confirmation number). The offer is limited to the Meditation Mastery teleseminar only, and your registration in the seminar is subject to availability of space and/or changes to the program schedule. The course must be completed by July 1, 2007. The value of this complimentary admission is $400 as of January 2006. Corporate or organizational purchasers may not use one book to invite more than two people. While participants will be responsible for the costs of calling, admission to the program is complimentary. Participants in the event are under no additional financial obligation whatsoever to Project Bliss or Mark Thornton. This offer is not connected to Sounds True, the publisher of the book. Project Bliss reserves the right to refuse admission to anyone it believes may disrupt the training.